BABYLON
Its History and Prophecies

by
David Hocking

BABYLON: Its History and Prophecies

Copyright 2015 by HFT Publications
PO Box 3927 Tustin, CA 92781
1-800-75-BIBLE

Printed in the United States of America

Unless noted otherwise, all Scripture is taken from The Holy Bible, King James Version, copyright 1982, by Thomas Nelson, Inc. Used by permission.

All rights reserved. No part of this publication may be reproduced, stored in a retrieval system, or transmitted in any form or by any means, electronic, mechanical, photocopying, recording, or otherwise, without the prior written consent of the Publisher.

ISBN   978-0-9882431-7-0

OUTLINE OF BOOK

SCRIPTURE – Isaiah 47:1-15	4
A BRIEF INTRODUCTION	5
Part I – HISTORY OF BABYLON	**9**
SEVEN THINGS about the origin of Babylon	20
Part II – KING OF BABYLON	**41**
SCRIPTURE – Isaiah 14:1-27 & Ezekiel 28:1-19	43
A BRIEF HISTORY OF TYRE	48
Part III – MYSTERY OF BABYLON	**63**
SCRIPTURE – Revelation 17:1-18	64
Part IV – FALL OF BABYLON	**93**
SCRIPTURE – Revelation 18:1-24	94
SOME FINAL THOUGHTS	117
BIBLIOGRAPHY	139

ISAIAH 47:1-15

"Come down, and sit in the dust, O virgin daughter of Babylon, sit on the ground: there is no throne, O daughter of the Chaldeans; for thou shalt no more be called tender and delicate. Take the millstones, and grind meal: uncover thy locks, make bare the leg, uncover the thigh, pass over the rivers. Thy nakedness shall be uncovered, yea, thy shame shall be seen: I will take vengeance, and I will not meet thee as a man. As for our Redeemer, the LORD of hosts is His Name, the Holy One of Israel. Sit thou silent, and get thee into darkness, O daughter of the Chaldeans: For thou shalt no more be called, The lady of kingdoms. I was wroth with My people, I have polluted Mine inheritance, and given them into thine hand: thou didst shew them no mercy; upon the ancient hast thou very heavily laid thy yoke. And thou saidst, I shall be a lady forever: so that thou didst not lay these things to thy heart, neither didst remember the latter end of it. Therefore hear now this, thou that art given to pleasures, that dwellest carelessly, that sayest in this heart, I am, and none else beside me; I shall not sit as a widow, neither shall I know the loss of children: But these two things shall come to thee in a moment in one day, the loss of children, and widowhood: they shall come upon thee in their perfection for the multitude of thy sorceries, and for the great abundance

of thine enchantments. For thou hast trusted in thy wickedness: thou hast said, None seeth me. Thy wisdom and thy knowledge, it hath perverted thee; and thou hast said in thine heart, I am, and none else beside me. Therefore shall evil come upon thee; thou shalt not know from whence it riseth: and mischief shall fall upon thee; thou shalt not be able to put it off: and desolation shall come upon thee suddenly, which thou shalt not know. Stand now with thine enchantments, and with the multitude of thy sorceries, wherein thou hast labored from thy youth; if so be thou shalt be able to profit, if so be thou mayest prevail. Thou art wearied in the multitude of thy counsels. Let now the astrologers, the stargazers, the monthly prognosticators, stand up, and save thee from the things that shall come upon thee. Behold, they shall be as stubble; the fire shall burn them; they shall not deliver themselves from the power of the flame: there shall not be a coal to warm at, nor fire to sit before it. Thus shall they be unto thee with whom thou hast labored, even thy merchants, from thy youth; they shall wander every one to his quarter; none shall save thee."

A BRIEF INTRODUCTION

Babylon is mentioned 286 times in the Bible of which 12 usages are found in the NT, six of those in the book of Revelation. The word "Babel" is used twice – Genesis 10:10 and 11:9.

Most of these references are referring to the massive and beautiful city of the Neo-Babylonian period (625-539 BC). With its "Hanging Gardens" and massive walls it has been regarded as one of the "Seven Wonders of the Ancient World." The Greek historian Herodotus (484-425 BC) reported upon visiting the site that its splendor surpassed any city of the known world.

It was also the capital of the 18th century BC King Hammurabi, and was known throughout history as a great center of culture and religion. It was Nebuchadnezzar II (605-562 BC) who brought Babylon to its glory as it was called "The Palace of Heaven and Earth, the Seat of Kingship." In Daniel 4:30 Nebuchadnezzar boasted *"Is not this great Babylon that I have built for the house of the kingdom by the might of my power, and for the honor of my majesty?"*

Ancient Babylon covered an area of 1000 acres making it the largest city of the ancient world, some 15% larger than Nineveh. It had 1179 temples and a population of over 100,000 but could easily have handled over 250,000 people. The famous "Ishtar Gate" was 70 feet high and its arched opening 15 feet wide. Babylon's most significant temple was Esagila ("the temple that raises its head") and was supposedly the home of the god Marduk. According to cuneiform documents the temple was surrounded by an enclosure of about 1410 feet by 720 feet and housed over 50 other temples and shrines. Interesting comment by Jeremiah (50:38): *"it is the land of graven images, and they are mad upon their idols."* Over 6000 figures (idols) were uncovered in the excavations of ancient Babylon and over 10 major altars. There were 180 open-air shrines for Ishtar and 200 identifiable places for other deities.

Adjacent to the temple of Esagila was the tower or ziggurat named Etemenanki called "the foundation house of heaven and earth." It measured about 300 feet square at the base and rose in seven stages to a height of 300 feet. It could very well have been reconstructed and restored from the original "Tower of Babel" mentioned in Genesis 11. The Babylonians believed it was built by the gods.

The very word *"Babylon"* has provoked enormous interest and fascination. In terms of Bible prophecies, it holds a major part of Biblical teachings. Next to the LORD Himself, and the 2566 references to the Nation of Israel, Babylon becomes a major subject of Bible prophecy both past and future.

Interest in Babylon's history increased at the time of the war called "Desert Storm." The late Saddam Hussein, ruler and dictator of Iraq, spent a great deal of time and money attempting to rebuild ancient Babylon and bring its past greatness and glory to Iraq once again. It did not happen, although a great deal of building did take place. The interest in Babylon has continued due to the many battles and conflicts that Iraq has experienced in modern times.

It is time to study the Biblical material more carefully, and discern the importance of Babylon in future events.

We begin with the study of the history of Babylon, charting its origin and historical events.

The HISTORY of BABYLON

Part I

THE HISTORY OF BABYLON

The Biblical story begins in Genesis 10:8-10 and 11:1-9:

"And Cush begat Nimrod: he began to be a mighty one in the earth. He was a mighty hunter before the LORD: wherefore it is said, Even as Nimrod the mighty hunter before the LORD. And the beginning of His kingdom was Babel, and Erech, and Accad, and Calneh, in the land of Shinar."

"And the whole earth was of one language, and of one speech. And it came to pass, as they journeyed from the east, that they found a plain in the land of Shinar; and they dwelt there. And they said one to another, Go to, let us make brick, and burn them throughly. And they had brick for stone, and slime had they for mortar. And they said, Go to, let us build us a city and a tower, whose top may reach unto heaven; and let us make us a name, lest we be scattered abroad upon the face of the whole earth. And the LORD came down to see the city and the tower, which the children of men builded. And the LORD said, Behold, the people is one, and they have all one language; and this they begin to do: and now nothing will be restrained from them, which they have imagined to do. Go to, let us go down, and there confound their language, that they may not understand one another's

speech. So the LORD scattered them abroad from thence upon the face of all the earth: and they left off to build the city. Therefore is the name of it called Babel; because the LORD did there confound the language of all the earth: and from thence did the LORD scatter them abroad upon the face of all the earth."

It should be obvious to readers of the Biblical story that the name of Babylon has been associated with rebellion and efforts to rule and conquer the world. Today we have witnessed the rise of radical Islam which continues to promote the idea and project of a "caliphate" or Islamic empire where Sharia law will be enforced. These forces of evil intent are putting together many Muslims (primarily) into a formidable army and their goal of establishing a Muslim empire in the Middle East does not end in that part of the world. They are dedicated to establishing another "Babylon" that will rule the entire world once again! They speak of their god with the name of "Allah" (which was one of the 360 deities of ancient Mecca). They have no sympathy for other religious beliefs, and they concentrate on the elimination of Jews and Christians from the planet. Ancient Babylon became an independent city-state in 1894 BC. The remains of the city exist in a place today called Hillah, about 85 kilometers (53 miles) south of Baghdad, between the Tigris and Euphrates Rivers. The original ancient city was built on the Euphrates River itself.

The ancient city was ruled by the First Amorite Babylonian Dynasty, the apparent successor of the Sumero-Akkadian city of Eridu. It apparently became known as a "holy city" at the time of Hammurabi, an Amorite king. As Babylon grew larger in population and power, the southern portions of Mesopotamia became known as Babylonia.

After many years and a rebuilding process by the Assyrians, Babylon became the seat of the Neo-Babylonian Empire from 608 BC to 539 BC, the year when Babylon was conquered by the Medo-Persian Empire. During the Neo-Babylonian era, the famous "Hanging Gardens of Babylon" were built and was eventually named as one of the Seven Wonders of the Ancient World (confirmed by Herodotus, the Greek historian who visited the location). After the fall of Babylon, it was ruled by the Achaemenid, Seleucid, Parthian, Roman and Sassanid empires.

Babylon figures prominently in the Biblical books of Genesis, Daniel, Jeremiah, and Isaiah, and most importantly, in the Book of Revelation. The German archaeologist, Robert Koldewey, was the first to excavate Babylon's ruins in 1899 AD

HOW OLD WAS BABYLON?

The earliest details as to the age of the city of Babylon come from Sargon of Akkad (known as Sargon the Great) who ruled from 2334 to 2279 BC. He claimed to have built temples at Babylon and referred to Babylon's large port on the Euphrates River. One interesting fact is that every ancient writer refers to Babylon with great respect and a sense of reverence for its religious impact upon the ancient world.

Babylon's most famous king of the old empire was Hammurabi (1792-1750 BC) who was known for his famous law codes. He enlarged the city and heightened the walls, and temples and canals. His administrative skills allowed him to unite all of Mesopotamia under the rule of Babylon, and by 1755 BC, Babylon was the largest city in the world and gave the name Babylonia to his empire in Mesopotamia.

Babylon was sacked by the Hittites in 1595 BC with very little resistance. The Kassites followed the Hittites and renamed the city Karanduniash. The Assyrians followed the Kassites. The Assyrian ruler Sennacherib (705 to 681 BC) responded to the revolt of Babylon to his leadership by sacking the city and scattering its ruins – he did this as an example to others. After being assassinated by his sons, his successor, Esarhaddon, re-built Babylon and returned it to its former glory. The city later revolted against Ashurbanipal of Nineveh who besieged and defeated the city but did not destroy it completely. The reputation of the city as a center of learning and culture was already well established by this time.

BIBLICAL BABYLON (Neo-Babylonian Empire)

After the fall of the Assyrian Empire in 612 BC, a Chaldean named Nabopolassar came to the throne of Babylon and through many alliances created what we now know as the Neo-Babylonian Empire. His son, Nebuchadnezzar II (604-561 BC) renovated and remodeled the city so that it covered 2200 acres of land and boasted of some of the most beautiful and impressive structures in all of Mesopotamia.

This city of Nebuchadnezzar stood in a broad plain and was an exact square. It was surrounded by a broad and deep moat which was full of water, behind which was a wall fifty royal cubits in width and 200 in height. The walls were 22 feet thick.

This was also the time of the Babylonian exile of the Jewish people and the time when the Babylonian Talmud was written. The Euphrates River divided the city in two between an "old" and a "new" city with the Temple of Marduk and the great towering Ziggurat in the center.

The Neo-Babylonian Empire continued under the influence of Nabonidus and his successor Belshazzar (mentioned in the Book of Daniel) until 539 BC when the Empire fell to the Persians under Cyrus the Great at the Battle of Opis.

The Persians continued to honor Babylon. Babylonian mathematics, cosmology, and astronomy were highly respected. When the Persian Empire fell to Alexander the Great in 331 BC, he did not allow his troops to damage the buildings nor molest the inhabitants.

By the time the Parthian Empire ruled in Mesopotamia in 141 BC, Babylon was deserted and somewhat forgotten. It was never restored to its former glory and prestige.

The oldest buildings of Babylon cannot be recovered. Its ruins are buried under the Euphrates River.

BABYLON'S PAGAN WORSHIP

The Sumerian supreme god was named Enlil, and as Babylon grew in power and influence, its unimportant city god, named Marduk, became the new supreme god who took over many of the attributes that were given to the original supreme god – Enlil. An expression developed that called Marduk "the Enlil of the gods." The famous Babylonian temple of

Marduk (named Esagila) and its ziggurat named Etemenanki was considered to be the "foundation of heaven and earth." In the creation epic Enuma Elis, Babylon is the center of the universe.

One of the evidences that Babylon was controlling the religious world was its annual New Year's Festival called "Akitu." The priests of Babylon taught that on this festival the gods left their cities and countries to visit Marduk, and announce their plans for the New Year.

During the days of the Assyrian Empire, the Assyrian kings spoke of themselves as kings of both Assyria and Babylon. It showed their respect for the Babylonian civilization. From Tiglath-Pileser III (744-727 BC) on, the Assyrian rulers wanted the world to know of their respect for the Babylonian civilization and its religious beliefs and practices.

The Babylonians, however, revolted under Marduk-apla-iddin in 703 BC (mentioned in the Bible as Merodach Baladan), and king Sennacherib sacked the city in 689 BC. This act involved a worldwide disappointment at Sennacherib's impiety. Babylon's population was deported to Nineveh and the site of ancient Babylon was abandoned for some time.

Finally, under the rule of King Esarhaddon (680-669 BC) the people of Babylon were allowed to return. One of the ancient documents says that "the gods had decreed that Babylon was to be in ruins for 70 years." But, Esarhaddon allowed the people to return after only 11 years.

The Assyrian king, Ashurbanipal (668-631 BC), tried to establish a new plan for ruling Babylon, and appointed his brother Samas-suma-ukin as king. However, he revolted and once again, Babylon was captured. Another brother served as king of Babylon, and in 627 BC, the Assyrian king sent two of his relatives to serve as governors. They were expelled by a Babylonian soldier named Nabopolassar who had fought once in the Assyrian army but now was starting a kingdom for himself.

In addition to the details mentioned above, it was 612 BC when the Babylonians along with the Medes attacked Nineveh and sacked the city, an historical event that allowed Babylon to once again become the capital of the Near East. But it was not long before the Persian king known as Cyrus the Great captured Babylon (539 BC), and appointed his son, Cambyses as king of Babylon.

Babylon was also the site where Alexander the Great died in 323 BC having no more worlds to conquer!

Babylon's greatest fame and importance in the annals of ancient history occurred under the leadership of Nebuchadnezzar, the son of Nabopolassar (605 BC). Nebuchadnezzar reigned for more than 40 years, and is prominent in the Bible as the ruler who destroyed Jerusalem in 586 BC, and carried the Jews into their Babylonian captivity.

The history of Babylon is indeed unique, and the Biblical connection quite dramatic as it relates to end-time events. To summarize the history of Babylon before we take a serious look at the Biblical facts regarding its origin, here is a basic timeline for the history of Babylon:

2350 BC	– First code of laws by Urukagina, king of Lagash
2000 BC	– Babylon controls Mesopotamia
1984 BC	– Amorite dynasty established in Babylon
1795-1750 BC	– Hammurabi, king of Babylon
1792 BC	– Hammurabi builds the walls of Babylon
1787 BC	– Hammurabi of Babylon conquers Uruk and Isin
1772 BC	– The Code of Hammurabi

1761 BC	–	Hammurabi destroys the city of Mari
1755 BC	–	Hammurabi rules Mesopotamia from Babylon
1595 BC	–	Hittites sack Babylon, ending Amorite rule
1595-1155 BC	–	Kassite dynasty rules over Babylon
1220 BC	–	Babylon under Assyrian control
853 BC	–	Babylon depends on Assyrian military support
750 BC	–	Network of aqueducts in Babylon
734 BC	–	Babylon captured by Chaldeans
729 BC	–	Babylon occupied by Assyrians
612 BC	–	Nineveh sacked and burned by Babylon & Medes
605-562 BC	–	Nebuchadnezzar II is King of Babylon
597 BC	–	Nebuchadnezzar captures Jerusalem

586 BC — Nebuchadnezzar destroys Jerusalem and its Temple

575 BC — Ishtar gate and great walls built in Babylon

539 BC — Fall of Babylon by Cyrus of Persia

485 BC — Babylon destroyed by Xerxes of Persia

323 BC — Alexander the Great dies in Babylon

321-64 BC — Seleucid dynasty rules Babylon & Mesopotamia

SEVEN THINGS ABOUT THE BIBLICAL ORIGIN OF BABYLON

Returning to our discussions of the history of Babylon, we are most interested in the Biblical origin of Babylon. As we examine the Biblical account in Genesis 10 and 11, we conclude seven things:

1. **IT WAS A <u>RESULT</u> OF AN ATTEMPT TO ESTABLISH A KINGDOM THAT WOULD REBEL AGAINST GOD'S AUTHORITY!**

The **PERSON** behind this effort

His name was "Nimrod" and it means "to revolt" or "to rebel" – a very fitting description of this ancient warrior! His wife's name was "Semiramis" – the first high priestess of the Babylonian mystery religion. Later in this book we will deal with the origin and influence of the Babylonian mystery religion upon all nations and religious systems.

In rabbinical literature, Nimrod is the prototype of a rebellious people. He is identified with Cush and with Amraphel, the name of the latter being interpreted as "he whose words are dark."

The **PARTNER** Nimrod had – "Semiramis"

She was known as the "Queen of Babylon," and the leader of Babylon's mystery religion. After the global flood which destroyed millions of people, the only survivors were Noah, his three sons, Shem, Ham, and Japheth, and their wives – eight souls (as I Peter 3:20 confirms). One of the sons of Ham was named Cush, and he was the father of Nimrod.

In the area of the Persian Gulf, mythologies speak of the "Land of the Seven Cities." These cities composed the world's first empire.

Tradition speaks of Semiramis as a native of Erech and involved in sexual practices, managing a well-known brothel.

Some legends have Semiramis raised by doves in the desert, born of the goddess Atargatis. Her first husband was said to be the governor of Nineveh. King Ninus of Babylon was captivated by her beauty, and after her first husband committed suicide, he married her. That may have been the first of his two biggest mistakes in judgment. The second came when Semiramis, now Queen of Babylon, convinced Ninus to make her "Regent for a Day." He did so, and on that day, she had him executed, and she took the throne.

The symbolism of a mother and her child is found throughout mythological literature, and it seems to dominate the pagan religions of the ancient world. One of the myths about Semiramis claims that she was Noah's granddaughter, and both the mother and the wife of Nimrod.

In Genesis 10:10 we read of the "land of Shinar," the Biblical name for lower Mesopotamia. We speak of the original civilization as "Sumeria" which name is derived from the name of Nimrod's wife Semiramis.

A rift between Nimrod and Semiramis apparently developed (according to mythological literature) over the birth of her illegitimate son who was called Tammuz. Nimrod was furious and threatened to expose her. She, however, devised a plot to overthrow Nimrod. At one of the pagan festivals of the New Year celebrations, she motivated a drug-crazed priesthood to sacrifice Nimrod himself and install her bastard son as king. Nimrod, according to legend, died a horrible death.

To insure her power and control, Semiramis was deified as the mother of a god, and was installed as "The Queen of Heaven" and was pictured in the constellation called "Cassiopeia." Legend says that Semiramis died after she reigned as Queen of Babylon for 102 years.

The POWER which he exercised

The Bible refers to Nimrod as a *"mighty one in the earth"* and *"a mighty hunter before* (or against) *the LORD."*

Biblical information regarding Nimrod is brief, but mythological literature fills in the blanks. Whether these facts are true or not cannot be substantiated or confirmed.

What we do know is that Nimrod is the son of Cush who is the son of Ham. Other sons of Cush include Mizraim (original name of Egypt), Phut (Libya), and Canaan, the father of the wicked, immoral people that were in the Land of Israel when Abraham came into the Land that God promised him (Genesis 12:6).

We also know that *"the beginning of his kingdom was Babel"* – and that the story of the Tower of Babel would be a part of the original facts of the city, culture, and religion of ancient Babylon. Rabbis refer to the Tower of Babel as "the house of Nimrod."

The **PROJECT** he undertook

The Bible speaks of *"the beginning of his kingdom was Babel"* – it quickly encompassed other cities within Mesopotamia.

We are told in Genesis 11 that the name of this tower or ziggurat was *"Babel"* and from Genesis 10:10 that the *"beginning"* of Nimrod's empire was this city. It would seem logical to identify Nimrod, therefore, with the building of this Tower. The name of the Tower was "Babel" which means "confusion" – the confusion that resulted from God changing the languages of the people who once lived there.

In several mythological legends Nimrod is pictured as one of the giants in stature. He was known as "The Subduer of Leopards" – he earned such fame (according to legend) by conquering large, wild animals.

2. It was a **REBELLION** against the command of the LORD!

After the global flood, the LORD gave a specific command to Noah in Genesis 9:1 - *"And God blessed Noah and his sons, and said unto them, Be fruitful, and multiply, and replenish the earth."* In Genesis 9:7 we again read of this important command: *"And you, be ye fruitful, and multiply; bring forth abundantly in the earth, and multiply therein."*

The rebellion of Nimrod and his people is made clear in Genesis 11:4 – *"And they said, Go to, let us build us a city and a tower, whose top may reach unto heaven; and let us make us a name, lest we be scattered abroad upon the face of the whole earth."*

Deuteronomy 1:26 reminds us that such rebellion was common among the people of God. It says, *"Notwithstanding ye would not go up, but rebelled against the commandment of the LORD your God."*

Genesis 10:9 – *"Even as Nimrod the mighty hunter before the LORD"* – the word *"before"* can also be translated as "against" and fits the context better.

3. It was a **REVOLT** against the worship of the LORD!

The LORD wants "altars of sacrifice" and not "towers of human achievement"! In Genesis 4:1-5 we read these words describing the worship that the LORD desires:

"And Adam knew Eve his wife; and she conceived, and bare Cain, and said, I have gotten a man from the LORD. And she again bare his brother Abel. And Abel was a keeper of sheep, but Cain was a tiller of the ground. And in process of time it came to pass, that Cain brought of the fruit of the ground an offering unto the LORD. And Abel, he also brought of the firstlings of his flock and of the fat thereof. And the LORD had respect unto Abel and to his offering; But unto Cain and to his offering he had not respect. And Cain was very wroth, and his countenance fell."

The question is, was there any evidence of sacrifice by killing a lamb previous to the above timing? Back in Genesis 3:21 we read: *"Unto Adam also and to his wife did the LORD God make coats of skins, and clothed them."*

This fact of being clothed with animal skins requires that animal sacrifices were made. In Genesis 8:20-21 we read:

"And Noah builded an altar unto the LORD; and took of every clean beast, and of every clean fowl, and offered burnt offerings on the altar. And the LORD smelled a sweet savor; and the LORD said in His heart, I will not again curse the ground any more for man's sake; for the imagination of man's heart is evil from his youth; neither will I again smite any more every thing living, as I have done."

Remember again that Nimrod was the son of Cush, and the great grandson of Noah. The issue of sacrifices on the altar had already been established both before and after the global flood.

The revolt of Nimrod's Babylon was specifically against the worship of the Lord. It is fascinating to fly over the southern portions of Mesopotamia and observe that 24 ziggurats have remains in the Mesopotamian valley! Genesis 11:1-4 reveals clearly that Babylon is all about revolting against the worship of the LORD:

"And the whole earth was of one language, and of one speech. And it came to pass, as they journeyed from the east, that they found a plain in the land of Shinar; and they dwelt there. And they said one to another, Go to, let

us make brick, and burn them throughly. And they had brick for stone, and slime had they for mortar. And they said, Go to, let us build us a city and a tower, whose top may reach unto heaven; and let us make us a name, lest we be scattered abroad upon the face of the whole earth."

We shall learn in our study of Babylon that it represents the revolt of the human heart against the true worship of the LORD. Human efforts are often a substitution for simple faith in God's sacrificial system. Salvation is NOT by works, but by faith in the finished work of the Messiah, including His death, burial, and resurrection! Babylon emphasizes human achievement and the worship of demonic forces and their false systems of worship.

4. It was a **RESPONSE** rooted in pride and the glorification of man!

Genesis 11:4 quotes them saying *"let us make us a name."*

Daniel 3:1 says: *"Nebuchadnezzar the king made an image of gold, whose height was threescore cubits, and the breadth thereof six cubits: he set it up in the plain of Dura, in the province of Babylon."*

Daniel 3:16-18 records that Shadrach, Meshach, and Abednego would not bow down and worship the golden image of Nebuchadnezzar. We read: *"Shadrach, Meshach, and Abednego answered and said to the king, O Nebuchadnezzar, we are not careful to answer thee in this matter. If it be so, our God Whom we serve is able to deliver us from the burning fiery furnace, and He will deliver us out of thine hand, O king. But if not, be it known unto thee, O king, that we will not serve thy gods, nor worship the golden image which thou hast set up."*

Of course, Nebuchadnezzar was filled with anger and fury, and the LORD God of Israel delivered the three Hebrew children.

We read of his pride in Daniel 4:28-30: *"All this came upon the king Nebuchadnezzar. At the end of twelve months he walked in the palace of the kingdom of Babylon. The king spake, and said, Is not this great Babylon, that I have built for the house of the kingdom by the might of my power, and for the honor of my majesty?"*

Immediately Nebuchadnezzar was struck by God, and a voice from heaven said: *"Thy kingdom is departed from thee."* He became like a beast of the field, but the good news is that at the end of his life, he repented and gave God the glory, as Daniel 4:37 says: *"Now I Nebuchadnezzar praise and extol and honor the King of heaven, all Whose works are* truth, and His ways judgment: and those that walk in pride He is able to abase."

One of the Hebrew words used of pride is *ga'on* and it often refers to an arrogant conceit that will incur the wrath of God. Proverbs 8:13 says: *"The fear of the LORD is to hate evil: pride, and arrogancy, and the evil way, and the forward mouth, do I hate."* Proverbs 16:18 says: *"Pride goeth before destruction, and an haughty spirit before a fall."*

Leviticus 26:19 – *"And I will break the pride of your power; and I will make your heaven as iron, and your earth as brass."*

Jeremiah 13:9 – *"Thus saith the LORD, After this manner will I mar the pride of Judah, and the great pride of Jerusalem."*

Hosea 5:5 – *"And the pride of Israel doth testify to his face: therefore shall Israel and Ephraim fall in their iniquity; Judah also shall fall with them."*

The LORD hates our pride and arrogance, and His judgment will fall upon all who respond to Him as though we do not need Him and can succeed without His help and power.

5. It was a **<u>REMINDER</u>** of God's control and sovereignty over all the events of human history!

Genesis 11:5-8 – *"And the LORD came down to see the city and the tower, which the children of men builded. And the LORD said, Behold, the people is one, and they have all one language; and this they begin to do: and now nothing will be restrained from them, which they have imagined to do. Go to, let us go down, and there confound their language, that they may not understand one another's speech. So the LORD scattered them abroad from thence upon the face of all the earth: and they left off to build the city."*

Psalm 103:19 – *"The LORD hath prepared His throne in the heavens; and His kingdom ruleth over all."*

Psalm 135:5-6 – *"For I know that the LORD is great, and that our Lord is above all gods. Whatsoever the LORD pleased, that did He in heaven, and in earth, in the seas, and all deep places."*

Daniel 2:20-22 – *"Daniel answered and said, Blessed be the Name of God forever and ever: for wisdom and might are His: And He changeth the times and the seasons: He removeth kings, and setteth up kings: He giveth wisdom unto the wise, and knowledge to them that know understanding. He revealeth the deep and secret things; He knoweth what is in the darkness, and the light dwelleth with Him."*

We are reminded of three powerful things about God in the beginnings of Babylon:

- (1) It reminds us of God's <u>KNOWLEDGE</u> of all that humanity does – Genesis 11:5 – *"the LORD came down to see the city and the tower, which the children of men builded."*

- (2) It reminds us of God's <u>MAJESTY</u> – Genesis 11:7 – *"let US go down"* – a statement that reveals the tri-unity of God Himself (Father, Son, and Holy Spirit).

- (3) It reminds us of God's <u>POWER</u> – Genesis 11:7 – *"and there confound their language, that they may not understand one another's speech."*

<u>NOTE:</u> In mythology (Sumerian 3rd dynasty of UR) – we learn that people once spoke one language until ENKI, the Sumerian god of wisdom, confounded their speech!

- (4) It reminds us of God's <u>PURPOSES</u> – Genesis 11:8-9 – *"so the LORD scattered them abroad from thence upon the face of all the earth"*

We should never forget the powerful words of God in Psalm 11:4 – *"The LORD is in His holy temple, the LORD's throne is in heaven: His eyes behold, His eyelids try, the children of men."*

6. It was a **REASON** for believers to resist all attempts to establish a world government and religion without God!

Psalm 9:17 states clearly: *"The wicked shall be turned into hell, and all the nations that forget God."*

In the Book of Revelation a woman rides a beast that has seven heads with ten horns on the seventh head. We are told in Revelation, that this symbolism is representing the kingdoms or empires of history. We read these words from Revelation 17:9-14:

"The seven heads are seven mountains, on which the woman sitteth. And there are seven kings (or kingdoms): five are fallen, and one is, and the other is not yet come; and when he cometh, he must continue a short space. And the beast that was, and is not, even he is the eighth, and is of the seven, and goeth into perdition. And the ten horns which thou sawest are ten kings, which have received no kingdom as yet; but receive power as kings one hour with the beast.

These have one mind, and shall give their power and strength unto the beast. These shall make war with the Lamb, and the Lamb shall overcome them: for He is LORD of lords, and KING of kings..." (more on these matters in Part III – the MYSTERY OF BABYLON)

Five world empires or kingdoms had already fallen in John's day (95 AD – date of writing the Book of Revelation).
    EGYPT
    ASSYRIA
    BABYLON
    MEDO-PERSIA
    GREECE

The one existing in John's day was, of course – ROME! Rome was the last attempt at a world empire. But, the Bible asserts that there is coming one more attempt to establish a world empire without belief and commitment to God Himself.

It should be obvious from Genesis 11 that it is not the will of God to have a one world government. It was, and is, and always has been, the will of God to scatter people into many different nations. Attempts at empires trying to unite people under a single banner have all collapsed in human history in God's timing and plans.

In recent history of the Middle East, we have a radical group of Muslims who desire to set up a "caliphate" or "Muslim Empire." The last such attempt was the Ottoman Empire which ruled for 400 years, but disintegrated after World War I. The radicals who want to establish Sharia law as binding upon all the people who live under their authority and rule, have become quite brutal – beheading people in public and on videos. They started their efforts in the middle of the wars that have developed in the Middle East. They first called themselves ISIL – standing for the Islamic State of Iraq and Levant (referring to Syria and Lebanon), then they changed to ISIS – Islamic State of Iraq and Syria.

Now, like all previous empires they call themselves simply IS – meaning an Islamic State – their goal is worldwide domination, a final empire that will establish Muslim theology and beliefs throughout the entire world.

In a sense, the League of Nations was an attempt at a world government. However, World War I diminished people's confidence, and in a few more years, we had the establishment of the United Nations. Its headquarters is in New York, and its members seem dominated by Muslim nations.

President George Bush, Sr. (father of George Walker Bush) was one of the first leaders in the modern world of the 20th century AD to call for a "New World Order." The battle of

"Desert Storm" brought together many nations and armies to fight Saddam Hussein and his forces who had invaded Kuwait.

We have also had a new dream and desire of European leaders to promote a world government among European nations and refer to themselves as the European Union.

Many of the promoters of world government are influenced by the United States of America. For years the population was opposed to any type of world government and many Christians who follow the Bible carefully were adamantly opposed to such a world political body. However, in the course of time as our world changes and our Christian culture diminishes in impact and importance to political leaders, we have seen many politicians and people of wealth who have rallied around the need for a world government that can bring peace to the planet. The Bible is clear in its prophetic plans that world peace can only be achieved by the coming of the Messiah of Israel, the Prince of peace!

The original intent of Nimrod and the Babylonian Empire he designed is still the great goal of many world leaders. Bible believing Christians still are opposed to such calls for world government and control, knowing what the Bible (specifically the Book of Revelation) warns concerning a worldwide deception that causes people to put their trust in world leaders who might be able by negotiations, treaties, and military conquests, to establish another world government as known by nations in past history.

7. It was a **REALIZATION** that salvation is based on faith in the Messiah of Israel, and not upon man-made religion and good works!

In the early history of Babylon, the literature is filled with religious beliefs and practices that dominated the culture and controlled the people. The "gods of Babylon" is a fascinating understanding of what people believe and practice when the LORD God of Israel is ignored and disobeyed. There are two major issues that dominate what is called *"abomination"* in Biblical history and prophecy – idolatry and immorality.

One of the greatest commentaries on human belief and behavior that ignores the God of the Bible is found in the Apostle Paul's letter to the Romans. Romans 1:18-32 cannot be improved in its analysis of what people do when they ignore and neglect the God of the Bible. This passage of Scripture reveals what happens to people who forsake the God of the Bible and His Word!

"For the wrath of God is revealed from heaven against all ungodliness and unrighteousness of men, who hold (suppress) the truth in unrighteousness; Because that which may be known of God is manifest in them; for God hath shewed it unto them. For the invisible things of Him from the creation of the world are clearly seen, being understood by the things that are made, even His eternal power and Godhead; so that they are without excuse: Because that, when they knew God, they glorified Him not as God, neither were thankful; but became vain in their imaginations, and their foolish heart was darkened. Professing themselves to be wise, they became fools, and changed the glory of the uncorruptible God into an image made like to corruptible man, and to birds, and fourfooted beasts, and creeping things. Wherefore God also gave them up to uncleanness through the lusts of their own hearts, to dishonor their own bodies between themselves: Who changed the truth of God into a lie, and worshipped and served the creature more than the Creator, Who is blessed forever. Amen.

For this cause God gave them up unto vile affections: for even their women did change the natural use into that which is against nature: And likewise also the men, leaving the natural use of the woman, burned in their lust one toward another; men with men working that which is unseemly, and *receiving in themselves that recompence of their error which was meet. And even as they did not like to retain God in their knowledge, God gave them over to a reprobate mind, to do those things which are not convenient; Being filled with all unrighteousness, fornication, wickedness, covetousness, maliciousness; full of envy, murder, debate, deceit, malignity; whisperers, backbiters, haters of God, despiteful, proud, boasters, inventors of evil things, disobedient to parents, without understanding, covenant-breakers, without natural affection, implacable, unmerciful: Who knowing the judgment of God, that they which commit such things are worthy of death, not only do the same, but have pleasure in them that do them."*

Romans 3:10-18 adds to the argument of Romans 1:18-32:

"As it is written, There is none righteous, no, not one: There is none that understandeth, there is none that seeketh after God. They are all gone out of the way, they are together become unprofitable; there is none that doeth good, no, not one. Their throat is an open sepulcher; with their tongues they have used deceit; the poison of asps is under their lips: Whose mouth is full of cursing and bitterness: Their feet are swift to shed blood: Destruction and misery are in their ways:

And the way of peace have they not known: There is no fear of God before their eyes."

The above analysis tells us the real story of Babylonianism and its influence upon human hearts.

Romans 6:23 – *"The wages of sin is death; but the gift of God is eternal life through Jesus Christ our Lord."*

Acts 4:12 – *"Neither is there salvation in any other: for there is none other name under heaven given among men, whereby we must be saved."*

Romans 10:9-13 – *"That if thou shalt confess with thy mouth the Lord Jesus, and shalt believe in thine heart that God hath raised Him from the dead, thou shalt be saved. For with the heart man believeth unto righteousness; and with the mouth confession is made unto salvation. For the scripture saith, Whosoever believeth on Him shall not be ashamed. For there is no difference between the Jew and the Greek: for the same Lord over all is rich unto all that call upon Him. For whosoever shall call upon the Name of the Lord shall be saved."*

The KING of BABYLON
Part II

THE KING OF BABYLON

Babylon has had some outstanding leaders, such as Nimrod, Hammurabi, Nebuchadnezzar II, and Cyrus the Persian. But, the Bible teaches that the real King of Babylon is SATAN, the devil himself!

Babylon, of course, has been a literal city and Babylonia, a literal empire in ancient times. But, the Bible reveals that there is a far more sinister plot behind Babylonianism, and that in fact, all nations of the world have been affected by its beliefs, teachings, and practices. Under the influence and powerful control of Satan, Babylon has been the direct antithesis to everything that represents God's plan for the human race, and His prophetic scriptures.

We are told in the Bible that Satan was once *"the anointed cherub"* who was created by God, but because of pride has fallen morally and in the future will be removed completely from having any access to God with his constant accusations and attacks upon believers.

Satan is called *"the devil"* and the angels that joined him in his rebellion against God are described as *"evil spirits"* and *"demons."*

I Peter 5:8 – *"Be sober, be vigilant; because your adversary the devil, as a roaring lion, walketh about, seeking whom he may devour."*

Revelation 12:9 – *"And the great dragon was cast out, that old serpent, called the Devil, and Satan, which deceiveth the whole world: he was cast out into the earth, and his angels were cast out with him."*

Revelation 9:11 calls him a *"king"* and the *"angel of the bottomless pit"* and he has a name of a "destroyer" – being called *Abaddon* in Hebrew and *Apollyon* in Greek.

There are two unique descriptions of Satan that reveal his diabolical plans in this world. In Isaiah 14:1-27 (listed below) – he is described in Isaiah 14:4 as the real *"king of Babylon."* In Ezekiel 28:12 the Bible refers to him as the *"king of Tyrus* (Tyre).*"* Take the time now to read these fascinating accounts!

ISAIAH 14:1-27

"For the LORD will have mercy on Jacob, and will yet choose Israel, and set them in their own land: and the strangers shall be joined with them, and they shall cleave to the house of Jacob. And the people shall take them, and bring them to their place: and the house of Israel shall possess them in the land of the LORD for servants and handmaids: and they

shall take them captives, whose captives they were; and they shall rule over their oppressors. And it shall come to pass in that day that the LORD shall give thee rest from thy sorrow, and from thy fear, and from the hard bondage wherein thou wast made to serve. That thou shalt take up this proverb against the KING OF BABYLON, and say, How hath the oppressor ceased! The golden city ceased! The LORD hath broken the staff of the wicked, and the sceptre of the rulers. He who smote the people in wrath with a continual stroke, he that ruled the nations in anger, is persecuted, and none hindereth. The whole earth is at rest, and is quiet: they break forth into singing. Yea, the fir trees rejoice at thee, and the cedars of Lebanon, saying, Since thou art laid down, no feller is come up against us. Hell from beneath is moved for thee to meet thee at thy coming: it stirreth up the dead for thee, even all the chief ones of the earth; it hath raised up from their thrones all the kings of the nations. All they shall speak and say unto thee, Art thou also become weak as we? Art thou become like unto us? Thy pomp is brought down to the grave, and the noise of thy viols: the worm is spread under thee, and the worms cover thee. How art thou fallen from heaven, O Lucifer, son of the morning! How art thou cut down to the ground, which didst weaken the nations!! For thou hast said in thine heart, I will ascend into heaven, I will exalt my throne above the stars of God: I will sit also upon the *mount of the congregation, in the sides of the north: I will ascend above the heights of the clouds; I will be like the most High. Yet thou shall be brought down to hell, to the sides of the pit. They that see thee, shall narrowly look upon thee, and consider thee, saying, Is this the man that made the earth to tremble, that did shake kingdoms; That made the world as a wilderness, and destroyed the cities thereof; that opened not the house of his prisoners? All the kings of the nations, even all of them, lie in glory, every one in his own house. But thou art cast out of thy grave like an abominable branch, and as the raiment of those that are slain, thrust through with a sword, that go down to the stones of the pit; as a carcase trodden under feet. Thou shalt not be joined with them in burial, because thou hast destroyed the land, and slain thy people: the seed of evildoers shall never be renowned. Prepare slaughter for his children for the iniquity of their fathers; that they do not rise, nor possess the land, nor fill the face of the world with cities. For I will rise up against them, saith the LORD of hosts, and cut off from BABYLON the name, and remnant, and son, and nephew, saith the LORD. I will also make it a possession for the bittern, and pools of water: and I will sweep it with the besom of destruction, saith the LORD of hosts. The LORD of hosts hath sworn, saying, Surely as I have thought, so shall it come to pass; and as I have purposed, so shall it stand: That I will break the*

Assyrian in My land, and upon My mountains tread him under foot: then shall his yoke depart from off them, and his burden depart from off their shoulders. This is the purpose that is purposed upon the whole earth: and this is the hand that is stretched out upon all the nations. For the LORD of hosts hath purposed, and who shall disannul it? and His hand is stretched out, and who shall turn it back?"

Clearly, Satan, described as *"Lucifer, son of the morning"* is the real KING OF BABYLON! We also have an important passage dealing with the identity of Satan in Ezekiel 28:1-19. Please take the time to read it.

EZEKIEL 28:1-19

"The word of the LORD came again unto me, saying, Son of man, say unto the PRINCE OF TYRUS, Thus saith the Lord GOD; Because thine heart is lifted up, and thou hast said, I am a God, I sit in the seat of God, in the midst of the sea; yet thou art a man, and not God, though thou set thine heart as the heart of God: Behold, thou art wiser than Daniel; there is no secret that they can hide from thee: With thy wisdom and with thine understanding thou hast gotten thee riches, and hast gotten gold and silver into thy treasures: By thy great wisdom and by thy traffic hast thou increased thy riches, and thine heart is lifted up because of thy riches:

Therefore thus saith the Lord GOD; Because thou hast set thine heart as the heart of God; Behold, therefore I will bring strangers upon thee, the terrible of the nations: and they shall draw their swords against the beauty of thy wisdom, and they shall defile thy brightness. They shall bring thee down to the pit, and thou shalt die the deaths of them that are slain in the midst of the seas. Wilt thou yet say before him that slayeth thee, I am God? but thou shalt be a man, and no God, in the hand of Him that slayeth thee. Thou shalt die the deaths of the uncircumcised by the hand of strangers: for I have spoken it, saith the Lord GOD. Moreover the word of the LORD came unto me, saying, Son of man, take up a lamentation upon the KING OF TYRUS, and say unto him, Thus saith the Lord GOD; Thou sealest up the sum, full of wisdom, and perfect in beauty. Thou hast been in Eden the garden of God; every precious stone was thy covering, the sardius, topaz, and the diamond , the beryl, the onyx, and the jasper, the sapphire, the emerald, and the carbuncle, and gold: the workmanship of thy tabrets and of thy pipes was prepared in thee in the day that thou was created. Thou art the anointed cherub that covereth; and I have set thee so: thou wast upon the holy mountain of God; thou hast walked up and down in the midst of the stones of fire. Thou was perfect in thy ways from the day that thou wast created, till iniquity was found in thee. By the multitude of thy merchandise they have filled the midst of thee with violence, and thou hast sinned: therefore I will cast thee as profane out of the mountain of God: and I will destroy thee, O covering cherub, from the midst of the stones of fire. Thine heart was lifted up because of thy beauty; thou hast corrupted thy wisdom by reason of thy brightness: I will cast thee to the ground; I will lay thee before kings, that they may behold thee. Thou hast defiled thy sanctuaries by the multitude of thine iniquities, by the iniquity of thy traffic; therefore will I bring forth fire from the midst of thee, it shall devour thee, and I will bring thee to ashes upon the earth in the sight of all them that behold thee. All they that know thee among the people shall be astonished at thee: thou shalt be a terror, and never shalt thou be anymore."

These two passages reveal the origin, fall, and infiltration of Satan into the kingdoms of Babylon and Tyre.

A BRIEF HISTORY OF TYRE

Tyre was an amazing city off the coast of present-day Lebanon. It was an economic power and it seemed indestructible to the nations of the world that spent money and time within her walls.

Tyre was an ancient Phoenician port city which was known as Europa (gave Europe its name). The name means "rock" and the city consisted of two parts: the main trade center was on an island and the older city was about a half mile away on the mainland. The older city was known by the name of Ushu and was founded in 2750 BC.

The prosperity of Tyre was noticed by Nebuchadnezzar II of Babylon who laid siege to this island fortress for thirteen years.

The people of Tyre were known as workers in dye from the shells of the Murex shellfish. This purple dye was greatly valued in the ancient world. The Greeks call this place "Phoinikes" which means "purple people."

According to the Bible, both the Apostle Paul and Jesus Himself visited the city. Tyre also had trade agreements with King David of Israel. The golden age of this island fortress began around the 10th century BC, and by the 8th century BC, Tyre was colonizing other sites in the area and enjoying great wealth and prosperity.

Tyre was also known for its pagan religious system that worshipped the god Melqart (who seems to be a deified version of Hercules). Baal and Ashtoreth were also worshipped by these Phoenicians. The name Melqart means "King of the City."

Most of the nations who did any business with Tyre were well aware of its fortress and the difficulty of trying to conquer it. It wasn't until the time of Alexander the Great in the 4th century BC that the city was conquered. After a seige of about seven months, Alexander took the city and massacred its 30,000 inhabitants.

Rome took the ruined city as a colony in 64 BC and built roads, monuments, and aquaducts which can still be seen today. In the 7th century AD, the city was taken by the Muslims.

THE PERSON BEHIND THE KING OF BABYLON

In Isaiah 14:12-15 it describes Satan and says:

"How art thou fallen from heaven, O Lucifer, son of the morning! How art thou cut down to the ground, which didst weaken the nations! For thou hast said in thine heart, I will ascend into heaven, I will exalt my throne above the stars of God; I will sit also upon the mount of the congregation, in the sides of the north: I will ascend above the heights of the clouds; I will be like the most High: Yet thou shalt be brought down to hell, to the sides of the pit."

This passage (Isaiah 14:4) is stated to be a proverb *"against the King of Babylon."*

The reference of LUCIFER

This is a play upon Canaanite religion. In Luke 10:17-20 Jesus made these remarkable statements to the seventy who joyfully said to him – *"Lord, even the devils are subject unto us through Thy Name."* Jesus said: *"I beheld Satan as lightning fall from heaven. Behold, I give unto you power to tread on serpents and scorpions, and over all the power of the enemy; and nothing shall by any means hurt you. Notwithstanding in this rejoice not, that the spirits are subject unto you; but rather rejoice because your names are written in heaven."* AMEN!

When Isaiah 14:12 says that Lucifer is the *"son of the morning"* it appears to be a direct prophecy against the devil and refers to Canaanite religion. The Hebrew word *helel* means "morning star." In Canaanite religion Helel and Ishtar attempted a heavenly coup that failed (according to Canaanite mythology).

The five "I WILL" statements of Satan appear to be a reminder of the Tower of Babel in Genesis 11:1-9 and a reminder of Genesis 3 when the devil told Eve that *"ye shall be as gods, knowing good and evil."*

In the text of Isaiah 14:13 we have the phrase *"in the sides of the north."* These words are translated by the Jewish Bible as *"on the summit of Zaphon"* which in Canaanite mythology was the abode of the gods. The New International Version of the Bible says *"on the utmost heights of the sacred mountain"* and the same thing is found in the text of Psalm 48:2 when it refers to the *"sides of the north"* or literally the *"summit of Zaphon."* Mount Zaphon is in northern Philistia and was considered to be the seat of Canaanite gods.

It is in Ezekiel 28:13-15 where we learn that Satan was *"the anointed cherub"* and the text says *"Thou wast perfect in thy ways from the day that thou wast created, till iniquity was found in thee."*

Satan is also called *"an angel of light"* in II Corinthians 11:14 where we read: *"And no marvel; for Satan himself is transformed into an angel of light."* Revelation 9:11 also refers to him as *"a king"* and calls him *"the angel of the bottomless pit"* and refers to him as *"Abaddon"* and *"Apollyon"* (terms which mean "destroyer.").

In John 8:44 Jesus called the devil *"a murderer from the beginning"* and said *"there is no truth in him."* Jesus said that he is *"the father of lies."*

I John 3:8 says of Satan: *"He that committeth sin is of the devil; for the devil sinneth from* the beginning. For this purpose the Son of God was manifested, that He might destroy the works of the devil."

I John 5:18 adds: *"We know that whosoever is born of God sinneth not; but he that is begotten of God keepeth himself, and that wicked one toucheth him not."*

Revelation 12:9 says that Satan *"deceiveth the whole world"* and the tool he has used throughout history is BABYLON!

HOW DOES SATAN SEDUCE AND DECEIVE US?

II Corinthians 11:3 says: *"But I fear, lest by any means, as the serpent beguiled Eve through his subtilty, so your minds should be corrupted from the simplicity that is in Christ."*

I Timothy 4:1 – *"Now the Spirit speaketh expressly, that in the latter times some shall depart from the faith, giving heed to seducing spirits, and doctrines of devils."*

    1. He <u>CASTS</u> doubt on God's Word!

Genesis 3:1 says: *"Now the serpent was more subtil than any beast of the field which the LORD God had made. And he said unto the woman, Yea, hath God said, Ye shall not eat of every tree of the garden?"* Satan knows what God has commanded, but in deceiving Eve he deliberately casts doubt on God's Word. He knew that God did not forbid Eve from eating from many of the trees – the command involved one tree.

When Eve answered she added to what the LORD had commanded, and that was the beginning of her compromise and downfall. She said *"God hath said, Ye shall not eat of it, neither shall ye touch it, lest ye died."* But, God did not say she could not touch it – she added that!

   2. He <u>CONTRADICTS</u> God's Word!

In Genesis 3:4 it says: *"And the serpent said unto the woman, Ye shall not surely die."*

   3. He <u>CHALLENGES</u> God's motives!

We read in Genesis 3:5 that the serpent told Eve: *"For God doth know that in the day ye eat thereof, then your eyes shall be opened, and ye shall be as gods, knowing good and evil."*

   4. He <u>CONFUSES</u> people with miraculous deeds!

The Apostle Paul warned us in II Thessalonians 2:9: *"Even him, whose coming is after the working of Satan with all power and signs and lying wonders."*

Jesus said in Matthew 24:24 – *"For there shall arise false Christs, and false prophets, and shall shew great signs and wonders; insomuch that, if it were possible, they shall deceive the very elect."*

    5. He <u>COUNTERFEITS</u> the work of God!

One of the most revealing passages about the seduction and deception of Satan is found in II Corinthians 11:13-15

"For such are false apostles, deceitful workers, transforming themselves into the apostles of Christ. And no marvel; for Satan himself is transformed into an angel of light. Therefore it is no great thing if his ministers also be transformed as the ministers of righteousness; whose end shall be according to their works."

WHAT IS SATAN ABLE TO DO?

This question is very important for us all to understand. Although Satan is not omnipotent, he does have great power to deceive. As Revelation 12:9 says – Satan *"deceiveth the whole world"* and his efforts have often been focused on government and religion.

In addition to his deceptions, Satan is continually accusing believers in the presence of God as the Book of Job clearly teaches. Revelation 12:10 says: *"for the accuser of our brethren is cast down, which accused them before our God day and night."* While Satan is the prosecuting attorney as it were, in the courtroom of heaven itself, according to the Bible, believers have a defense attorney – Jesus Christ the righteous One! Romans 8:34 teaches: *"Who is he that condemneth? It is Christ that died, yea rather, that is risen again, Who is even at the right hand of God, Who also maketh intercession for us."* The Apostle John wrote in I John 2:1-2 – *"My little children, these things write I unto you, that ye sin not. And if any man sin, we have an advocate* (defense attorney) *with the Father, Jesus Christ the righteous: And He is the propitiation for our sins: and not for ours only, but also for the sins of the whole world."*

Satan tempts us to follow the lusts of the flesh instead of walking in obedience to God and His Word. In John 8:44 Jesus said to the religious leaders of His day: *"Ye are of your father the devil, and the lusts of your father ye will do. He was a murderer from the beginning, and abode not in the truth, because there is no truth in him. When he speaketh a lie, he speaketh of his own: for he is a liar, and the father of it."*

I Corinthians 7:5 warns married couples not to hold back from each other in meeting sexual needs: *"Defraud ye not one the other, except it be with consent* (mutual consent) *for a time, that ye may give yourselves to fasting and prayer; and come together again, that Satan tempt you not for your incontinency* (lack of control)." The devil knows our human weaknesses and he tempts us in the area of sexual need.

Ephesians 2:1-3 lays out an important strategy in dealing with the devil: *"And you hath He quickened, who were dead in trespasses and sins; Wherein in time past ye walked according to the course of this world, according to the prince of the power of the air, the spirit that now worketh in the children of disobedience: Among whom also we all had our conversation in times past in the lusts of our flesh and of the mind; and were by nature the children of wrath, even as others."*

One of the devil's great deceptions is to make us believe that God is tempting us to sin. But, James 1:13-15 says: *"Let no man say when he is tempted, I am tempted of God: for God cannot be tempted with evil, neither tempteth He any man: But every man is tempted, when he is drawn away of his own lust, and enticed. Then when lust hath conceived, it bringeth forth sin: and sin, when it is finished, bringeth forth death."*

Satan is the one blinding the minds of unbelievers as well as hindering the work of believers. In II Corinthians 4:3-4 we read: *"But if our gospel be hid, it is hid to them that are lost: In whom the god of this world hath blinded the minds of them which believe not, lest the light of the glorious gospel of Christ, Who is the image of God, should shine unto them."* That's what he is able to do to non-believers. I Thessalonians 2:18 adds: *"Wherefore we would have come unto you, even I Paul, once and again; but Satan hindered us."*

One of the strategies of the devil is to devour your confidence in the LORD and His purposes, especially when we suffer.

I Peter 5:8 says: *"Be sober, be vigilant; because your adversary the devil, as a roaring lion, walketh about, seeking whom he may devour."*

In summarizing what he is able to do:

1. He deceives the whole world!
2. He accuses the believers!
3. He tempts us to follow the lusts of the flesh!

WHAT CAN WE DO ABOUT IT?

1. We can <u>REALIZE</u> the <u>PURPOSE</u> of God in allowing Satanic attacks!

The Apostle Paul was suffering greatly by a *"thorn in the flesh"* and calls it *"the messenger of Satan to buffet me, lest I should be exalted above measure."* He begged the Lord to take this affliction out of his life, but God answered him in II Corinthians 12:9 and said: *"My grace is sufficient for thee: for My strength is made perfect in weakness."* Paul then said: *"Most gladly therefore will I rather glory in my infirmities, that the power of Christ may rest upon me. Therefore I take pleasure in infirmities, in reproaches, in necessities, in persecutions, in distresses for Christ's sake: for when I am weak, then am I strong."*

Peter spoke powerfully about what to do when Satan causes us not to understand the afflictions that God allows us to experience. I Peter 5:8-11 say:

"Be sober, be vigilant; because your adversary the devil, as a roaring lion, walketh about, seeking whom he may devour; whom resist stedfast in the faith, knowing that the same afflictions are accomplished in your brethren that are in the world. But the God of all grace, Who hath called us unto His eternal glory by Christ Jesus, after that ye have suffered a while, make you perfect, stablish, strengthen, settle you. To Him be glory and dominion forever and ever. Amen!"

    2. We can (and should) <u>RELY</u> upon the intercessory <u>PRAYER</u> of Jesus Christ!

Hebrews 7:24-25 says: *"But this Man, because He continueth ever, hath an unchangeable priesthood. Wherefore He is able to save them to the uttermost that come unto God by Him, seeing He ever liveth to make intercession for them."*

In John 17:15 in the prayer of Jesus to His Father in heaven He said: *"I pray not that Thou shouldest take them out of the world, but that Thou shouldest keep them from the evil (one)."*

   3. We can <u>RECOGNIZE</u> the <u>PROTECTION</u> of God's armor!

Ephesians 6:11 says: *"Put on the whole armor of God, that ye may be able to stand against the wiles* (methods and/or strategies) *of the devil."* In verse 16 we read: *"Above all, taking the shield of faith, wherewith ye shall be able to quench all the fiery darts of the wicked* (one).*"*

   4. We should <u>REMEMBER</u> the <u>PROMISE</u> of God if we resist the devil!

James 4:7 says: *"Submit yourselves therefore to God. Resist the devil, and he will flee from you."*

   5. We must <u>RESPOND</u> to the <u>PRESENCE</u> and <u>POWER</u> of the Holy Spirit!

I John 4:4 states clearly: *"Greater is He that is in you, than he that is in the world."*

The real KING of BABYLON was and is SATAN himself! He was the one deceiving that immediate post-flood generation, convincing them to build a tower instead of sacrificing on an altar of worship to God. Satan blasted them by indwelling Nimrod and his wife Semiramis – whom Satan convinced that she was the "Queen of Babylon" and could set up a pagan religious system that would challenge the Person and commands of Almighty God. She accepted the seduction of Satan (as did Eve in the Garden of Eden) and began to question all that she had heard from the survivors of the flood – Noah, his sons, and their wives.

BABYLON is still with us – don't be deceived into thinking that it faded into the walls of history – no more evident or real. No, it is still with us, and the Bible makes it clear (as we shall develop in the next part of our study). Satan's deceptions have penetrated all nations of human history – the governments of the world who are motivated by Satan to conquer and control the peoples of this world. The religious systems clearly are controlled by Satan and his vast army of demonic forces.

Satan's strategy has always been to question God and His Word and to suggest that God is really undermining your freedom to do whatever you want to do. Idolatry and immorality dominate our planet. Freedom without understanding of God's laws and purposes leads us into moral decay and anarchy and a serious bondage to self and sin.

The MYSTERY of BABYLON

Part III

THE MYSTERY OF BABYLON

One of the most interesting aspects of the study of Babylon is the Bible's reference to it in the Book of Revelation.

Revelation 17:1-18

"And there came one of the seven angels which had the seven vials (bowls), and talked with me, saying unto me, Come hither; I will shew unto thee the judgment of the great whore that sitteth upon many waters: With whom the kings of the earth have committed fornication, and the inhabitants of the earth have been made drunk with the wine of her fornication. So he carried me away in the spirit into the wilderness: and I saw a woman sit upon a scarlet colored beast, full of names of blasphemy, having seven heads and ten horns. And the woman was arrayed in purple and scarlet color, and decked with gold and precious stones and pearls, having a golden cup in her hand full of abominations and filthiness of her fornication: And upon her forehead was a name written, MYSTERY, BABYLON THE GREAT, THE MOTHER OF HARLOTS AND ABOMINATIONS OF THE EARTH. And I saw the woman drunken with the blood of the saints, and with the blood of the martyrs of Jesus: and when I saw her, I wondered with great admiration. And the angel said unto me, Wherefore didst thou

marvel? I will tell thee the mystery of the woman, and of the beast that carrieth her, which hath the seven heads and ten horns. The beast that thou sawest was, and is not; and shall ascend out of the bottomless pit, and go into perdition: and they that dwell on the earth shall wonder, whose names were not written in the book of life from the foundation of the world, when they behold the beast that was, and is not, and yet is. And here is the mind which hath wisdom. The seven heads are seven mountains, on which the woman sitteth. And there are seven kings: five are fallen, and one is, and the other is not yet come; and when he cometh, he must continue a short space. And the beast that was, and is not, even he is the eighth, and is of the seven, and goeth into perdition. And the ten horns which thou sawest are ten kings, which have received no kingdom as yet; but receive power as kings one hour with the beast. These have one mind, and shall give their power and strength unto the beast. These shall make war with the Lamb, and the Lamb shall overcome them: for He is LORD of lords, and KING of kings: and they that are with him are called, and chosen, and faithful. And he saith unto me, the waters which thou sawest, where the whore sitteth, are peoples, and multitudes, and nations, and tongues. And the ten horns which thou sawest upon the beast, these shall hate the whore, and shall make her desolate and naked, and shall eat her flesh, and burn her with fire. For God *hath put in their hearts to fulfill His will, and to agree, and give their kingdom unto the beast, until the words of God shall be fulfilled. And the woman which thou sawest is that great city, which reigneth over the kings of the earth."*

WHAT IS A "MYSTERY"?

The Greek word *musterion* is simply transliterated (said into English) rather than translated. It carries with its usage the following facts:

1. It refers to that which is hidden
2. It refers to that which is a secret
3. It refers to that which is not yet known but will one day be revealed

The Bible uses the term frequently (about 30 times). In the Aramaic sections of the Book of Daniel, the Aramaic word *raz* is used 9 times and refers to the dreams of King Nebuchadnezzar. In Daniel 2:28, Daniel said: *"But there is a God in heaven that revealeth secrets, and maketh known to the king Nebuchadnezzar what shall be in the latter days."*

In the New Testament the word used is *musterion.* When a person reads the Greek word *musterion* in English, it is simply the word "mystery."

Paul refers to the *"mystery of Christ"* in Ephesians 3:4, and speaks of the *"mystery"* that was to be known *"among the Gentiles"* which is *"Christ in you, the hope of glory (Colossians 1:27)."* He again refers to it in his letter to the Romans (Romans 16:25-26). Paul also refers to the *"mystery"* that *"blindness in part is happened to Israel, until the fullness of the Gentiles be come in* (Romans 11:25)." Also, in I Corinthians 15:51-52 he speaks of the *"mystery"* that not every believer will die, but all *"shall be changed."* He speaks also in Ephesians 1:9 of the *"mystery of His will"* and in Ephesians 3:9 of the *"fellowship of the mystery."*

The Apostle John refers to the *"mystery"* of *the "seven stars"* and the *"seven golden candlesticks"* in Revelation 1:20. He speaks also of the *"mystery of the woman"* whom he refers to as *"Mystery, Babylon the Great, the Mother of harlots and abominations of the earth"* in Revelation 17.

IS "BABYLON THE GREAT" THE SAME IN REVELATION 17 AND 18?

Bible scholars and teachers throughout the history of the church have questioned the relationship of BABYLON in Revelation 17-18. Two primary views have emerged in all the studies of Revelation:

1. Revelation 17 & 18 are talking about the same thing!

2. Revelation 17 is the religious Babylon and Revelation 18 is the commercial and political side of the city!

Consider the following facts:

1. Revelation 14 uses the term *"Babylon"* and says in verse 8 – *"And there followed another angel, saying, Babylon is fallen, is fallen, that great city, because she made all nations drink of the wine of the wrath of her fornication."*

In identifying Babylon that will fall, it is identified as a "woman" and uses the words *"she"* and *"her"* and the prediction is the same as the words of Revelation 18:2-3.

2. In describing BABYLON we are told that the *"kings of the earth"* have *"committed fornication"* with her and drink the *"wine of her fornication"* – Revelation 14:8; 17:2; 18:3, 9.

3. Revelation 17:16 pictures the destruction of the *"woman"* by the *"ten horns"* on the *"beast."* The Bible separates the *"beast"* from the *"woman"* who rides the beast.

4. In describing the fall of Babylon in Revelation 18:21-24 we read that *"in her was found the blood of prophets, and of saints, and of all that were slain upon the earth."*

5. In Revelation 19:1-2 the rejoicing of much people in heaven is over the destruction of *"the great whore."*

6. The use of feminine pronouns throughout both chapters seem to favor seeing that Babylon the Great is, in fact, the woman that rides the beast and her destruction is being pictured and predicted.

HOW SHOULD WE INTERPRET THE WORDS OF REVELATION 17:18 – "THAT GREAT CITY"?

This is one of the difficulties in interpreting the "MYSTERY OF BABYLON" in Revelation 17 & 18. The word *"Babylon"* is used in the Book of Revelation a total of six times:

> Revelation 14:8 – *"And there followed another angel, saying, Babylon is fallen, is fallen, that great city, because she made all nations drink of the wine of the wrath of her fornication."*

Revelation 16:19 – "And <u>the great city</u> was divided into three parts, and the cities of the nations fell: and <u>great Babylon</u> came in remembrance before God, to give unto her the cup of the wine of the fierceness of His wrath."

Revelation 17:5 – "And upon her forehead was a name written, MYSTERY, <u>BABYLON THE GREAT</u>, THE MOTHER OF HARLOTS AND ABOMINATIONS OF THE EARTH."

Revelation 18:2 – "And he cried mightily with a strong voice, saying, <u>Babylon the great</u> is fallen, is fallen, and is become the habitation of devils, and the hold of every foul spirit, and a cage of every unclean and hateful bird."

Revelation 18:10 – "Standing afar off for the fear of her torment, saying, Alas, alas <u>that great city Babylon</u>, that mighty city! For in one hour is thy judgment come."

Revelation 18:21 – "And a mighty angel took up a stone like a great millstone, and cast it into the sea, saying, Thus with violence shall <u>that great city Babylon</u> be thrown down, and shall be found no more at all."

Babylon is called the *"great city"* in Revelation 14:8; 16:19; 18:10; and 18:21. The term *"great city"* is also used in the Book of Revelation to refer to Jerusalem in Revelation 11:8 *"And their dead bodies* (two witnesses) *shall lie in the street of the <u>great city</u>, which spiritually is called Sodom and Egypt, where also our Lord was crucified."* The words *"great city"* are also found in Revelation 21:10 *"And he carried me away in the spirit to a great and high mountain, and shewed me <u>that great city</u>, the holy Jerusalem, descending out of heaven from God."*

When we put all of the passages together, it would appear that the following possibilities concerning the identity of Babylon as the *"great city"* need to be examined carefully:

1. It refers to the city of Jerusalem! Revelation 11:8

The problem with this view is the failure of Jerusalem to be associated with the merchants of the sea.

2. It refers to a rebuilt city of Babylon!

A few Bible teachers take this position, and when the late Saddam Hussein started such a project, many thought this would lead to a correct interpretation. However, his project did not succeed. Some of those who hold this view point to the gigantic embassy that the United States has built.

> 3. It refers to an unknown city of the tribulation period – the coming day of the LORD to planet earth!

Of course, this is possible – we simply have no present evidence to this fact. Also, the Bible's account of Babylon seems to suggest that it is a great city that has existed throughout history.

> 4. It refers to the city of ROME!

Most of the reformers during the Protestant Reformation held this view. Some said the Roman Pope was also the Antichrist; others spoke of the Pope as the False Prophet of Revelation 13.

In modern times, the late Dave Hunt wrote an excellent commentary entitled "A WOMAN RIDES THE BEAST" and gave a strong argument for the city being ROME. In Revelation 18:24 we read: *"And in her was found the blood of prophets, and of saints, and of all that were slain upon the earth."*

In the book by Alexander Hislop (1858 AD) entitled "THE TWO BABYLONS" he makes a serious case for Babylon being the Roman Catholic Church. Its history has been submerged in the Babylonianism of ancient Babylon, and its practices have continued to perpetuate and promote the beliefs and practices of Babylonianism.

THE GREAT HARLOT
Revelation 17:1-6

"And there came one of the seven angels which had the seven vials, and talked with me, saying unto me, Come hither; I will shew unto thee the judgment of the great whore that sitteth upon many waters: With whom the kings of the earth have committed fornication, and the inhabitants of the earth have been made drunk with the wine of her fornication. So he carried me away in the spirit into the wilderness: and I saw a woman sit upon a scarlet colored beast, full of names of blasphemy, having seven heads and ten horns. And the woman was arrayed in purpose and scarlet color, and decked with gold and precious stones and pearls, having a golden cup in her hand full of abominations and filthiness of her fornication: And upon her forehead was a name written, MYSTERY, BABYLON THE GREAT, THE MOTHER OF HARLOTS AND ABOMINATIONS OF THE EARTH. And I saw the woman drunken with the blood of the saints, and with the blood of the martyrs of Jesus: and when I saw her, I wondered with great admiration."

The **ANNOUNCEMENT** of judgment – 17:1b
"I will shew unto thee the judgment of the great whore that sitteth upon many waters"

In Revelation 16:19 we read of the coming judgment upon Babylon as it says: *"and great Babylon came in remembrance before God, to give unto her the cup of the wine of the fierceness of His wrath."*

In Revelation 19:2 we read of the praises of *"much people in heaven (v. 1)"* who say: *"For true and righteous are His judgments: for He hath judged the great whore, which did corrupt the earth with her fornication, and hath avenged the blood of His servants at her hand."*

The **AUTHORITY** of the woman – 17:1-3, 15
"sitteth upon many waters"

Revelation 17:15 – *"And he saith unto me, The waters which thou sawest, where the whore sitteth, are peoples, and multitudes, and nations, and tongues."*

Revelation 18:3 – *"For <u>all</u> nations have drunk of the wine of the wrath of her fornication, and the kings of the earth hath committed fornication with her, and the merchants of the earth are waxed rich through the abundance of her delicacies."*

The **APPEARANCE** of the woman – 17:4
"And the woman was arrayed in purple and scarlet color, and decked with gold and precious stones and pearls, having a golden cup in her hand full of abominations and filthiness of her fornication."

1. Notice the **APPAREL** of the woman – *"arrayed in purple and scarlet color"* – picturing royalty – the first woman of Babylon was Semiramis, the wife of Nimrod who was known as the "Queen of Babylon."

Revelation 18:7 says: *"How much she hath glorified herself, and lived deliciously, so much torment and sorrow give her: for she saith in her heart, I sit a queen, and am no widow, and shall see no sorrow."*

2. Notice the **ADORNMENT** of this woman – *"decked with gold and precious stones and pearls"*

Revelation 18:16 says *"And saying, Alas, alas, that great city, that was clothed in fine linens, and purple, and scarlet, and decked with gold, and precious stones, and pearls!"*

3. Notice the **ABOMINATIONS** of this woman *"having a golden cup in her hand full of abominations and filthiness of her fornication"*

Jeremiah 51:6-8 speaks of Babylon as a harlot woman:

"Flee out of the midst of Babylon, and deliver every man his soul: be not cut off in her iniquity; for this is the time of the LORD's vengeance; He will render unto her a recompence. Babylon hath been a golden cup in the LORD's hand, that made all the earth drunken: the nations have drunken of her wine; therefore the nations are mad. Babylon is suddenly fallen and destroyed: howl for her; take balm for her pain, if so be she may be healed."

The <u>ASSOCIATION</u> of this woman with Babylon 17:5 – *"And upon her forehead was a name written, MYSTERY, BABYLON THE GREAT, THE MOTHER OF HARLOTS AND ABOMINATIONS OF THE EARTH."*

Babylon is mentioned 286 times in the Bible – its ruins located about 20 miles south of present-day Baghdad.

There are many associations with Babylon that are historical practices affecting the religions of the world, including Christianity.

> 1. The <u>SYMBOLISM</u> of the mother and child

The roots of such beliefs are definitely connected with Babylon and its mystery religions.

> BABYLON – Semiramus and Tammuz
> ASIA – Cybele and Desius
> INDIA – Isi and Iswara
> EGYPTIANS – Isis and Horus (Osiris)
> ITALIANS – Venus and Cupid
> GRECIANS – Aphrodite and Eros

Many Bible teachers and scholars have pointed out that all of the above beliefs are Satan's deceptions and counterfeits drawing people from the Biblical truth of the Jewish virgin (Miriam – Mary) who bore the Messiah, our blessed Lord Yeshua (Isaiah 7:14 cf. Matthew 1:22-25).

In 1825 AD, Pope Leo XII struck a medal with his image on one side, and of the woman with a golden cup in her right hand on the other side – which in his view represented the Roman Catholic Church.

> 2. The <u>SIMILARITY</u> of Christian celebrations with the practices of Babylonianism

CHRISTMAS

From a Jewish point of view, our Lord Yeshua was probably born on Rosh Hashanah (September 29, 2 BC) – the December 25th day comes from pagan sources, not the facts of the Bible. The use of Christmas trees, lights, candles, giving of gifts, and, of course, the promotion of Santa Claus – all have their origin in pagan practice.

With regard to the real facts about the birth of Jesus:

> HEROD – died on January 14, 1 BC
> AUGUSTUS CAESAR – died on August 19, 14 AD
> TERTULLIAN – birth of Jesus 41 years after Augustus began his rule
> IRENAEUS – disciple of Polycarp – Jesus was born in the 41st year of the reign of AUGUSTUS
> ZECHARIAH – father of John the Baptist – the priestly course of Abia – 8th division – John was born April 19-20, 2 BC (Passover) – six months before Jesus – which would be September 29, 2 BC – Rosh HaShanah!

Christmas being celebrated on December 25 has no connection whatsoever with the Biblical account of the birth of our Lord. Long before the Christian era, a festival was celebrated among the heathen that happened every December 25, honoring the birth of the son of the Babylonian Queen of Heaven – Semiramis! That Christmas was originally a pagan festival is beyond all doubt. Calling it "Yule-day" reminds us of the Chaldee name for an "infant" or "little child" and the night that preceded it (which we call "Christmas Eve") was called "Mother-night" and it all referred to Babylonianism. The Church adopted many of these pagan festivals to encourage more pagans to join them in their beliefs and practices. The truth is that no such festival as Christmas was ever heard of in the churches until the 3rd century AD, and it wasn't until the 4th century AD that it gained any observance.

EASTER

Easter which supposedly celebrates the resurrection of our Lord Jesus Christ is nothing more that the worship of Astarte, one of the titles of the Queen of Heaven. On Assyrian monuments, the name is Ishtar, from which we get the pagan practice of Easter.

Socrates, the ecclesiastical historian said of Rome's celebration of Easter: "Thus much already laid down may seem a sufficient treatise to prove that the celebration of the feast of Easter began everywhere more of custom than by any commandment either of Christ or any Apostle." We should all know that the word "Easter" in Acts 12:4 refers not to any Christian festival, but to the Jewish Passover. This is one of the few places in our Bibles where the translators show an undue bias.

LENT

The practice of the 40 days of Lent is also not a Biblical teaching but rather another practice absorbed from Babylonianism. The teaching about the abstinence of Lent brought into the Church such corruption and superstition that one wonders why the people did not rise up against it when it was first proposed. It was at a Council held at Aurelia in 519 AD (time of Hormisdas, Bishop of Rome) which decreed that Lent should be solemnly kept before Easter.

BUNS AND EGGS

The "hot cross buns" of Good Friday, and the dyed eggs of Easter Sunday, were also Chaldean rites and were used in the worship of the Queen of Heaven, the goddess Easter (Ishtar) at least 1500 years before the Christian era.

In Jeremiah 7:17-18 we read: *"Seest thou not what they do in the cities of Judah and in the streets of Jerusalem? The children gather wood, and the fathers kindle the fire, and the women knead their dough, to make cakes to the Queen of Heaven, and to pour out drink offerings unto other gods, that they may provoke Me to anger."*

There are many papal instructions throughout Roman Catholic history that are indeed taken from Babylonianism and certainly not from the Bible. For example, in the Canon of the Mass, it is said: *"Oh blessed fault, which didst procure such a Redeemer!"* This statement was referring to the sin of our first parent, Eve. The idea behind it comes from Babylonianism and is purely pagan. It amounts to saying, "Thanks be to Eve, to whose sin we are indebted for the glorious Savior!" It is an idea utterly opposed to the true gospel. Even Augustine used many of these pagan sentiments and never got entirely delivered from them.

3. The <u>SACRIFICE</u> of the Mass

In the 4th century AD, the Queen of Heaven (under the name of Mary, the mother of Jesus) was beginning to be worshipped in the Christian Church. Epiphanius states that "the practice of offering and eating an "unbloody sacrifice" began with the women of Arabia, and at that time it was well known to have been adopted and originated from the pagans. The very shape of it (small thin, round wafer) came from pagan sources, originating in Babylonianism (picturing the sun). In the great temple of Babylon, the golden image of the Sun was exhibited for the worship of the Babylonian people.

4. The <u>SIGN</u> of the cross

Most people know that the "sign of the cross" is evidence that the individual is Roman Catholic in belief and practice. Politicians do it in public, some military do it as well, and most often, professional and collegiate athletes do it. It seems to them to be something like a "rabbit's foot" or a lucky charm of some sort. The magic virtues attributed to the so-called "sign of the cross" have no relationship to any Biblical teaching. Some priests say that this is what the Apostle Paul means when he said in Galatians 6:14: *"But God forbid that I should glory, save in the cross of our Lord Jesus Christ, by whom the world is crucified unto me, and I unto the world."*

The same sign of the cross that Rome now worships was also used in the Babylonian Mystery Religion. That which is now called the Christian cross was originally no Christian emblem at all, but was the mystic Tau of the Chaldeans and Egyptians – the initial "T" was referring to Tammuz of the Babylonian religion. That mystic Tau was marked in baptism on the foreheads of those initiated into the "Mysteries" of the Babylonian religion. In Babylon, the mystic Tau, as the symbol of great divinity was called "the sign of life." It was used as an amulet over the heart, and it was marked on the official garments of the priests of Rome. The vestal virgins of pagan Rome wore it suspended from their necklaces, as the Roman Catholic nuns do today. The Egyptians did the same as did many of the barbaric nations who came in contact with the Egyptian religion. There is hardly any pagan tribe where the cross has not been found as a prominent and important symbol of reverence and worship. The cross was worshipped by pagan Celts long before the incarnation and death of Christ.

The cross was widely worshipped in pagan religions and regarded as a sacred symbol. It was the symbol of Bacchus, the Babylonian Messiah, who was represented with a head-band covered with crosses.

In the office of the cross, it is called the "Tree of Life" and worshippers are taught to address it with these words: "Hail, O Cross, triumphal wood, true salvation of the world, among trees there is none like thee in leaf, flower, and bud. O Cross, our only hope, increase righteousness to the godly and pardon the offences of the guilty." In the London Record of April, 1842, these so-called "devotions" included these words: "O faithful cross, thou peerless tree, No forest yields the like of thee, Leaf, flower, and bud: Sweet is the wood, and sweet the weight, And sweet the nails that penetrate Thee, thou sweet wood."

Many Catholics do it, believing that it contains some sort of merit before God. No prayer can be said or act of worship without the sign of the cross on the part of a given individual.

Needless to say, a cross of wood or metal has no more efficacy or power than a pile of dirt. For individuals to make the sign of the cross upon themselves also is not only without merit or God's grace and forgiveness, it is quite frankly, an abomination in the sight of the Lord Himself.

The power belongs to the One Who was crucified on that Roman cross, and it is His death and resurrection upon which we place our hope of everlasting life.

Two things are major issues concerning this woman who rides the beast:

1. She is a **MYSTERY**!

2. She is a **MOTHER**!

The **ACCUSATION** against this woman – 17:6

"And I saw the woman drunken with the blood of the saints, and with the blood of the martyrs of Jesus: and when I saw her, I wondered with great admiration."

Revelation 18:24 – *"And in her was found the blood of prophets, and of saints, and of all that were slain upon the earth."*

In Revelation 17:6 we have the statement – *"with the blood of the martyrs of Jesus."* That means that the identity of the woman in John's day must be based on the future from the time of the Lord Jesus.

THE IDENTITY OF THE BEAST UPON WHICH THE WOMAN RIDES

Revelation 17:7-14 – *"And the angel said unto me, Wherefore didst thou marvel? I will tell thee the mystery of the woman, and of the beast that carrieth her, which hath the seven heads and ten horns. The beast that thou sawest was, and is not; and shall ascend out of the bottomless pit, and go into perdition: and they that dwell on the earth shall wonder, whose names were not written in the book of life from the foundation of the world, when they behold the beast that was, and is not, and yet is. And here is the mind which hath wisdom. The seven heads are seven mountains, on which the woman sitteth. And there are seven kings: five are fallen, and one is, and the other is not yet come; and when he cometh, he must continue a short space. And the beast that was, and is not, even he is the eighth, and is of the seven, and goeth into perdition. And the ten horns which thou sawest are ten kings, which have received no kingdom as yet; but receive power as kings one hour with the beast. These have one mind, and shall give their power and strength unto the beast. These shall make war with the Lamb, and the Lamb shall overcome them: for he is LORD of lords, and KING of kings; and they that are with Him are called, and chosen, and faithful."*

The story about the beast actually begins in Revelation 12:3-4 – *"And there appeared another wonder in heaven; and behold a great red dragon, having seven heads and ten horns, and seven crowns upon his heads. And his tail drew the third part of the stars of heaven, and did cast them to the earth: and the dragon stood before the woman* (picture of Israel) *which was ready to be delivered, for to devour her child as soon as it was born."*

The BEAST with seven heads and ten horns is described as *"a great red dragon."* It is a clear reference to Satan – Revelation 12:9 says: *"And the great dragon was cast out, that old serpent* (Genesis 3), *called the Devil, and Satan, which deceiveth the whole world; he was cast out into the earth, and his angels were cast out with him."* This event refers to the *"war in heaven"* mentioned in Revelation 12:7-8 – *"And there was war in heaven: Michael and his angels fought against the dragon; and the dragon fought and his* angels, and prevailed not; neither was their place found any more in heaven."

We begin with a great red DRAGON which the Bible describes as Satan and the Devil. The next reference is in Revelation 13:1 – *"And I stood upon the sand of the sea, and saw a beast rise up out of the sea, having seven heads and ten horns, and upon his horns ten crowns, and upon his heads the name of blasphemy."*

This description of the beast continues in Revelation 13:2-9:
"And the beast which I saw was like unto a leopard, and his feet were as the feet of a bear, and his mouth as the mouth of a lion: and the dragon (Satan) gave him his power, and his seat (throne), and great authority. And I saw one of his heads as it were wounded to death; and his deadly wound was healed: and all the world wondered after the beast. And they worshipped the dragon which gave power unto the beast: and they worshipped the beast, saying, Who is like unto the beast? Who is able to make war with him? And there was given unto him a mouth speaking great things and blasphemies; and power was given unto him to continue forty and two months. And he opened his mouth in blasphemy against God, to blaspheme His Name, and His tabernacle, and them that dwell in heaven. And it was given unto him to make war with the saints, and to overcome

them: and power was given him over all kindreds, and tongues, and nations. And all that dwell upon the earth shall worship him, whose names are not written in the book of life of the Lamb slain from the foundation of the world. If any man have an ear, let him hear."

THE <u>DESCRIPTION</u> OF THE BEAST

1. A man who comes out of the nations (Gentile) and receives his power and authority from Satan.

2. The beast has seven heads and ten horns.

3. The beast comes out of the abyss, the bottomless pit, where Satan and his angels are located. (Revelation 17:8)

4. He is like a leopard, a bear, and a mouth of a lion. (Daniel 7)

5. One of his heads (presumably the sixth head) received a deadly wound that would be healed in the future.

6. Five of the seven heads were no longer in existence in John's day – they are kings or kingdoms.
        EGYPT
        ASSYRIA

BABYLON
MEDO-PERSIA
GREECE

7. It would appear that the sixth head that did exist in John's day represents ROME! (Rome fell in 476 AD)

8. It appears that the 7th head is the one with ten horns – and speaks of a future confederacy.

9. The eighth head will come out of the previous seven! (Daniel 7:8)

Daniel refers to this coming world leader as a *"little horn"* that comes up in the midst of a ten nation confederacy, and quickly gains ascendency and authority.

It appears from the Bible facts we have that this coming world leader is the same as the coming ANTICHRIST!

Some teach that the *"heads"* are referring to individual Roman Emperors – but the facts do not teach this. The woman who rides the beast has been given a name – MYSTERY, BABYLON THE GREAT AND THE MOTHER OF HARLOTS AND ABOMINATIONS.

The *"beast"* appears to represent world empires that have existed in previous history. If our interpretations are correct, the *"beast"* is picturing all the nations of the world, and the woman is the one who continues to seduce them.

The final world empire appears to be a confederacy of *"ten horns"* that seem to be on the 7th head – an attempt at another world empire. The *"ten horns"* could represent ten nations of the end times, or perhaps more likely ten divisions of the world government that will come into existence. Out of this confederacy will arise the *"little horn"* or the ANTICHRIST himself, empowered by Satan.
His control and influence over the peoples of the world will be utterly amazing!

It appears that this coming confederacy will make war against the believers. Revelation 17:14 says: *"These shall make war with the Lamb, and the Lamb shall overcome them: for He is LORD of lords, and KING of kings."* In Revelation 13:7-8 we read: *"And it was given unto him to make war with the saints, and overcome them: and power was given him over all kindreds, and tongues, and nations.
And all that dwell upon the earth shall worship him, whose names are not written in the book of life of the Lamb slain from the foundation of the world."*

The DESTRUCTION of the woman
Revelation 17:16-18

"And the ten horns which thou sawest upon the beast, these shall hate the whore, and shall make her desolate and naked, and shall eat her flesh, and burn her with fire. For God hath put in their hearts to fulfill His will, and to agree, and give their kingdom unto the beast, until the words of God shall be fulfilled. And the woman which thou sawest is that great city, which reigneth over the kings of the earth."

Jeremiah 50:45-46 – "Therefore hear ye the counsel of the LORD that He hath taken against Babylon; and His purposes, that He hath purposed against the land of the Chaldeans: Surely the least of the flock shall draw them out: surely He shall make their habitation desolate with them. At the noise of the taking of Babylon the earth is moved, and the cry is heard among the nations."

Jeremiah 51:6-9 – "Flee out of the midst of Babylon, and deliver every man his soul: be not cut off in her iniquity; for this is the time of the LORD's vengeance; He will render unto her a recompence. Babylon hath been a golden cup in the LORD's hand that made all the earth drunken: the nations have drunken of her wine; therefore the nations are mad. Babylon is suddenly fallen and destroyed: howl for her, take balm for her pain, if so be she may be healed. We would have healed Babylon, but she is not healed: forsake her, and let us go everyone into his own country:

for her judgment reacheth unto heaven, and is lifted up even to the skies."

The FALL of BABYLON
Part IV

THE FALL OF BABYLON

Revelation 18:1-24

"And after these things I saw another angel come down from heaven, having great power; and the earth was lightened with his glory. And he cried mightily with a strong voice, saying, Babylon the great is fallen, is fallen, and is become the habitation of devils, and the hold of every foul spirit, and a cage of every unclean and hateful bird. For all nations have drunk of the wine of the wrath of her fornication, and the kings of the earth have committed fornication with her, and the merchants of the earth are waxed rich through the abundance of her delicacies. And I heard another voice from heaven, saying, Come out of her, My people, that ye be not partakers of her sins, and that ye receive not of her plagues. For her sins have reached unto heaven, and God hath remembered her iniquities. Reward her even as she rewarded you, and double unto her double according to her works: in the cup which she hath filled fill to her double. How much she hath glorified herself, and lived deliciously, so much torment and sorrow give her: for she saith in her heart, I sit a queen, and am no widow, and shall see no sorrow. Therefore shall her plagues come in one day, death, and mourning, and famine; and she shall be *utterly burned with fire: for strong is the Lord God Who judgeth her. And the kings of the earth, who have committed fornication and lived deliciously with her, shall bewail her, and lament for her, when they shall see the smoke of her burning. Standing afar off for the fear of her torment, saying, Alas, alas that great city Babylon, that mighty city! For in one hour is thy judgment come. And the merchants of the earth shall weep and mourn over her; for no man buyeth their merchandise anymore. The merchandise of gold, and silver, and precious stones, and of pearls, and fine linen, and purple, and silk, and scarlet, and all thyine wood, and all manner vessels of ivory, and all manner vessels of most precious wood, and of brass, and iron, and marble, And cinnamon, and odors, and ointments, and frankincense, and wine, and oil, and fine flour, and wheat, and beasts, and sheep, and horses, and chariots, and slaves, and souls of men. And the fruits that thy soul lusted after are departed from thee, and all things which were dainty and goodly are departed from thee, and thou shalt find them no more at all. The merchants of these things, which were made rich by her, shall stand afar off for the fear of her torment, weeping and wailing, and saying, Alas, alas, the great city, that was clothed in fine linen, and purple, and scarlet, and decked with gold, and precious stones, and pearls! For in one hour so great riches is come to nought. And every ship-master, and* all the company in ships, and sailors, and as many as trade by sea, stood afar off, and cried when they saw the smoke of her burning, saying, What city is like unto this great city! And they cast dust on their heads, and cried, weeping and wailing, saying, Alas, alas, that great city, wherein were made rich all that had ships in the sea by reason of her costliness! For in one hour is she made desolate. Rejoice over her, thou heaven, and ye holy apostles and prophets; for God hath avenged you on her. And a mighty angel took up a stone like a great millstone, and cast it into the sea, saying, Thus with violence shall that great city Babylon be thrown down, and shall be found no more at all. And the voice of harpers, and musicians, and of pipers, and trumpeters, shall be heard no more at all in thee; and no craftsman, of whatsoever craft he be, shall be found any more in thee; and the sound of a millstone shall be heard no more at all in thee; And the light of a candle shall shine no more at all in thee; and the voice of the bridegroom and of the bride shall be heard no more at all in thee: for thy merchants were the great men of the earth; for by thy sorceries were all nations deceived. And in her was found the blood of prophets, and of saints, and of all that were slain upon the earth."

ARGUMENTS for Babylon being the harlot woman in Revelation 17 and 18

1. The usage of the word *"Babylon"* – never used of the beast or its heads.

2. The context before and after Revelation 18.

    > **Revelation 16:19** – *"And the great city was divided into three parts, and the cities of the nations fell: and great Babylon came in remembrance before God to give unto her the cup of the wine of the fierceness of His wrath."*

    > **Revelation 19:2** – *"For true and righteous are His judgments: for He hath judged the great whore, which did corrupt the earth with her fornication, and hath avenged the blood of His servants at her hand."*

3. The statements of Revelation 6:9-11 with 17:6 and 18: 24

    > **Revelation 6:9-11** – *"And when he had opened the fifth seal, I saw under the altar the souls of them that were slain for the word of God, and for the testimony which they held: And they cried with a loud voice, saying, How long, O Lord, holy and true, dost Thou not judge and avenge our blood on*

them that dwell on the earth? And white robes were given unto every one of them; and it was said unto them, that they should rest yet for a little season, until their fellow-servants also and their brethren, that should be killed as they were, should be fulfilled."

Revelation 17:6 – *"And I saw the woman drunken with the blood of the saints, and with the blood of the martyrs of Jesus; and when I saw her, I wondered with great admiration."*

Revelation 18:24 – *"And in her was found the blood of prophets, and of saints, and of all that were slain upon the earth."*

RESULTS of the fall of Babylon

Isaiah 13:19-22 – *"And Babylon, the glory of kingdoms, the beauty of the Chaldees' excellency, shall be as when God overthrew Sodom and Gomorrah. It shall never be inhabited, neither shall it be dwelt in from generation to generation: neither shall the Arabian pitch tent there; neither shall the shepherds make their fold there. But wild beasts of the desert shall lie there; and their houses shall be full of doleful creatures; and* owls shall dwell there, and satyrs shall dance there. And the wild beasts of the islands shall cry in their desolate houses, and dragons in their pleasant palaces: and her time is near to come; and her days shall not be prolonged."

Jeremiah 51:36-37 – "Therefore thus saith the LORD; Behold, I will plead thy cause, and take vengeance for thee; and I will dry up her sea, and make her springs dry. And Babylon shall become heaps, a dwellingplace for dragons, an astonishment, and an hissing, without an inhabitant."

Jeremiah 51:41-44 – "How is Sheshach taken! And how is the praise of the whole earth surprised! How is Babylon become an astonishment among the nations! The sea is come up upon Babylon: she is covered with the multitude of the waves thereof. Her cities are a desolation, a dry land, and a wilderness, a land wherein no man dwelleth, neither doth any son of man pass thereby. And I will punish Bel in Babylon, and I will bring forth out of his mouth that which he hath swallowed up: and the nations shall not flow together any more unto him: yea, the wall of Babylon shall fall."

Jeremiah 51:47-49 – "Therefore, behold, the days come, that I will do judgment upon the graven images of Babylon: and her whole land shall be confounded, and all her slain shall fall in the midst of her. Then the heaven and the earth, all that is therein, shall sing for Babylon: for the spoilers shall come unto her from the north, saith the LORD. As Babylon hath caused the slain of Israel to fall, so at Babylon shall fall the slain of all the earth."

Jeremiah 51:53-55 – "Though Babylon should mount up to heaven, and thou she should fortify the height of her strength, yet from Me shall spoilers come unto her, saith the LORD. A sound of a cry cometh from Babylon, and great destruction from the land of the Chaldeans: Because the LORD hath spoiled Babylon, and destroyed out of her the great voice; when her waves do roar like great waters, a noise of their voice is uttered."

Jeremiah 51:64 – "And thou shalt say, Thus shall Babylon sink, and shall not rise from the evil that I will bring upon her: and they shall be weary. Thus far are the words of Jeremiah."

The **REASON** for the fall of Babylon

Revelation 18:3 – "For all nations have drunk of the wine of the wrath of her fornication, and the kings of the earth have committed fornication with her, and the merchants of the earth are waxed rich through the abundance of her delicacies."

1. The <u>EXTENT</u> of her influence – *"all nations have drunk of the wine of her fornication"*

2. The <u>EXPLANATION</u> of her seduction – *"and the kings of the earth have committed fornication with her"*

3. The <u>EFFECT</u> of her seductive ways – *"the merchants of the earth are waxed rich through the abundance of her delicacies"*

Babylon is a religious system which has dominated and controlled all nations of the earth!

The "<u>CUP</u>" in the woman's hand

Revelation 14:8-11 – *"And there followed another angel, saying, Babylon is fallen, is fallen, that great city, because she made all nations drunk of the wine of the wrath of her fornication. And the third angel followed them, saying with a loud voice, If any man worship the beast and his image, and receive his mark in his forehead, or in his hand, The same shall drink of the wine of the wrath of God, which is poured out without mixture into the cup of His indignation; and he shall be tormented with fire and brimstone in the presence of the holy angels, and in the presence of the Lamb: And the smoke of their torment ascendeth up forever and ever: and they have no rest day nor night, who worship the beast and his image, and whosoever receiveth the mark of his name."*

The word in Hebrew for "cup" is the word *"kos"* and is translated "cup" about 30 times, sometimes referring to a literal cup, and at other times, it has a metaphorical meaning. The word can be used in a positive sense, indicating Divine blessings, or abundant blessings from God.

But, the word "cup" refers symbolically to the outpouring of God's judgment and wrath upon those who rebel against Him. For example:

Psalm 11:6 – *"Upon the wicked He shall rain snares, fire and brimstone, and an horrible tempest: this shall be the portion of their CUP."*

Psalm 75:8 – *"For in the hand of the LORD there is a CUP and the wine is red; it is full of mixture; and He poureth out of the same: but the dregs thereof, all the wicked of the earth shall wring them out, and drink them."*

The woman's "cup" is revealed in the Bible to be filled with the *"wine of her fornication."*

Babylon and the Cup of God's Judgment

Jeremiah 25:12-17 – *"And it shall come to pass, when seventy years are accomplished, that I will punish the king of Babylon, and that nation, saith the LORD, for their iniquity, and the land of the Chaldeans, and will make it perpetual desolations. And I will bring upon that land all My words which I have pronounced against it, even all that is written in this book, which Jeremiah hath prophesied against all the nations. For many nations and great kings shall serve themselves of them also: and I will recompense them according to their deeds, and according to the works of their own hands. For thus saith the LORD God of Israel unto me; Take the wine cup of this fury at My hand, and cause all the nations, to whom I send thee, to drink it. And they shall drink, and be moved, and be mad, because of the sword that I will send among them. Then took I the CUP at the LORD's hand, and made all the nations to drink, unto whom the LORD had sent me."*

The phrase *"the CUP of the LORD's right hand"* is also found in Habakkuk 2:16.

Jeremiah 51:7-9 – *"Babylon hath been a golden CUP in the LORD's hand, that made all the earth drunken: the nations have drunken of her wine therefore the nations are mad. Babylon is suddenly fallen and destroyed: howl for her; take balm for her pain, if so be she may be healed. We would have healed*

Babylon, but she is not healed: forsake her, and let us go everyone into his own country: for her judgment reacheth unto heaven, and is lifted up even to the skies."

Revelation 17:4b says: *"having a golden CUP in her hand full of abominations and filthiness of her fornication."*

In that CUP which the woman has in her hand we have a powerful picture of God's wrath. The CUP contains *"the wine of the wrath of her fornication."* The Bible teaches that all nations have drunk of that wine!

The power of God's judgment is expressed clearly in Revelation 18:8b – *"for strong is the Lord God Who judgeth her."*

The <u>REMOVAL</u> of God's people

Revelation 18:4-5 – *"And I heard another voice from heaven, saying, Come out of her, My people, that ye be not partakers of her sins, and that ye receive not of her plagues. For her sins have reached unto heaven, and God hath remembered her iniquities."*

The word translated *"reached"* could very well be a play on words. The word is used of putting bricks together with mortar – perhaps in remembering the Tower of Babel.

God has remembered all the sins of Babylon! In Revelation 16:19 we read: *"and great Babylon came in remembrance before God, to give unto her the cup of the wine of the fierceness of His wrath."*

Jeremiah 51:6 – "Flee out of the midst of Babylon, and deliver every man his soul: be not cut off in her iniquity; for this is the time of the LORD's vengeance; He will render unto her a recompence."

The <u>RECOMPENCE</u> that Babylon will receive

Revelation 18:6-8 – "Reward her even as she rewarded you, and double unto her double according to her works: in the cup which she hath filled fill to her double. How much she hath glorified herself, and lived deliciously, so much torment and sorrow give her: for she saith in her heart, I sit as a queen, and am no widow, and shall see no sorrow. Therefore shall her plagues come in one day, death, and mourning, and famine; and she shall be utterly burned with fire: for strong is the Lord God Who judgeth her."

Jeremiah 51:29 – "And the land shall tremble and sorrow: for every purpose of the LORD shall be performed against Babylon, to make the land of Babylon a desolation without an inhabitant.

Jeremiah 51:37 – *"And Babylon shall become heaps, a dwelling place for dragons, an astonishment, and an hissing, without an inhabitant."*

Jeremiah 51:44 – *"And I will punish Bel in Babylon, and I will bring forth out of his mouth that which he hath swallowed up: and the nations shall not flow together anymore unto him: yea, the wall of Babylon shall fall."*

Jeremiah 51:47-49 – *"Therefore, behold, the days come, that I will do judgment upon the graven images of Babylon: and her whole land shall be confounded, and all her slain shall fall in the midst of her. Then the heaven and the earth, and all that is therein, shall sing for Babylon: for the spoilers shall come unto her from the north, saith the LORD. As Babylon hath caused the slain of Israel to fall, so at Babylon shall fall the slain of all the earth."*

The <u>RECIPIENTS</u> of the judgment of Babylon - Revelation 18:9-19

1. The KINGS of the earth – vv. 9-10

"And the kings of the earth, who have committed fornication and lived deliciously with her, shall bewail her, and lament for her, when they shall see the smoke of her burning. Standing afar off for the fear of her

torment, saying, Alas, alas that great city Babylon, that mighty city: for in one hour is thy judgment come."

All kings of the earth throughout history from the original empire of Nimrod and Semiramis until today have been seduced and deceived by the religion of Babylon.

2. The MERCANTS of the earth – vv. 11-16

"And the merchants of the earth shall weep and mourn over her; for no man buyeth their merchandise any more: The merchandise of gold, and silver, and precious stones, and of pearls, and fine linen, and purple, and silk, and scarlet, and all thyine wood, and all manner vessels of ivory, and all manner vessels of most precious wood, and of brass, and iron, and marble, and cinnamon, and odors, and ointments, and frankincense, and wine, and oil, and fine flour, and wheat, and beasts, and sheep, and horses, and chariots, and slaves, and souls of men. And the fruits that thy soul lusted after are departed from thee, and all things which were dainty and goodly are departed from thee, and thou shalt find them no more at all. The merchants of these things, which were made rich by her, shall stand afar off for the fear of her torment, weeping and wailing. And saying, Alas, alas, that great city, that was clothed in

fine linen, and purple, and scarlet, and decked with gold, and precious stones, and pearls!"

As often is the case throughout church history, the facts of Revelation 18 are difficult to connect with the major cities of the world. The text says *"the merchants of the earth"* and necessitates a city that could attract such merchandising and sales. For almost 2000 years, the attempt to identify "Babylon the Great" with a given city of the world has led to difficulties that at times seem insurmountable. This has led some Bible teachers and scholars to abandon completely any possible literal interpretation. Those who call themselves "preterists" (Latin word meaning "past") continue to insist that this Book of Revelation was written before 70 AD (no proof whatsoever!) and the fulfillment of it was seen in the destruction of Jerusalem by Roman armies in 70 AD. The interesting fact is the connection with Rome which at the time was certainly a "great city" and a "mighty city" – which controlled the then known world.

3. The sailors who traded by sea – vv. 17-19

"For in one hour so great riches is come to nought. And every shipmaster, and all the company in ships, and sailors, and as many as trade by sea, stood afar off, and cried

when they saw the smoke of her burning, saying, What city is like unto this great city! And they cast dust on their heads, and cried, weeping and wailing, saying, Alas, alas, that great city, wherein were made rich all that had ships in the sea by reason of her costliness! For in one hour is she made desolate."

Several issues arise from these words about the "sailors" who traded with the woman known as "Babylon the Great." One issue comes from the words *"all the company in ships, and sailors, and as many as trade by sea."* This city would have to be a major port doing trade with the world. A second issue that arises from Revelation 18 is the clear prediction that *"in one hour is she made desolate."* If the city is the *"great city"* and does all this business with the world, it must be of considerable size.

Back at the end of chapter 16 we learned that it was a *"great earthquake, such as was not since men were upon the earth, so mighty an earthquake, and so great."* When that earthquake hits, the Bible says that *"every island fled away, and the mountains were not found."* We also read in Revelation 16:21 that a *"great hail out of heaven"* fell upon men. These hailstones weighed about 100 pounds each – incredible!

But we also read in Revelation 17:16 – *"And the ten horns which thou sawest upon the beast, these shall hate the whore, and shall make her desolate and naked, and shall eat her flesh, and burn her with fire."* Then, in Revelation 18:8 we read: *"Therefore shall her plagues come in one day, death, and mourning, and famine; and she shall be utterly burned with fire: for strong is the Lord God Who judgeth her."* Revelation 18:10 says of this *"mighty city"* that *"in one hour is thy judgment come."* Again, in Revelation 18:17 we read *"For in one hour so great riches is come to nought."* Again in verse 19 it says: *"for in one hour is she made desolate."*

It appears that when Babylon the Great is destroyed, it happens quickly (the use of the phrase *"one hour"*) and the following events will occur to accomplish it:

>**THE BURNING OF THE CITY BY THE TEN NATION CONFEDERACY** (destroyed by the 7th head of the *"beast"* upon which the woman rides)
>
>**THE GREATEST EARTHQUAKE IN HUMAN HISTORY** (an event that causes *"the cities of the nations"* to fall)
>
>**THE GREAT HAILSTONES OUT OF HEAVEN**

The involvement of the LORD GOD Himself in this great disaster is clearly an issue – Revelation 18:8 – *"for strong is the Lord God Who judgeth her."*

Psalm 148:8 says: *"Fire, and hail; snow, and vapors; stormy wind fulfilling His word."*

The REJOICING of heaven's inhabitants
Revelation 18:20

"Rejoice over her, thou heaven, and ye holy apostles and prophets; for God hath avenged you on her."

This praise comes from not only the apostles and prophets who were the *"foundation of the church"* but the *"martyrs"* of history (Revelation 6:9-11), which would include those of the tribulation period, and the entire church composed of Jews and Gentiles who were raptured before the tribulation began. All *"heaven"* breaks out in praise to God over the destruction of the great harlot **"Babylon the Great."**

The complete REMOVAL of Babylon the Great   Revelation 18:21-24

"And a mighty angel took up a stone like a great millstone, and cast it into the sea, saying, Thus with violence shall that great

city Babylon be thrown down, and shall be found no more at all. And the voice of harpers, and musicians, and of pipers, and trumpeters, shall be heard no more at all in thee; and no craftsman of whatsoever craft he be, shall be found any more in thee; and the sound of a millstone shall be heard no more at all in thee; And the light of a candle shall shine no more at all in thee; and the voice of the bridegroom and of the bride shall be heard no more at all in thee: for thy merchants were the great men of the earth; for by thy sorceries were all nations deceived. And in her was found the blood of prophets, and of saints, and of all that were slain upon the earth."

1. It will come as a violent <u>CATASTROPHE</u>! *"with violence shall that great city be thrown down"*

Jeremiah 51:63-64 prophesies: *"And it shall be, when thou hast made an end of reading this book, that thou shalt bind a stone to it, and cast it into the midst of Euphrates: And thou shalt say, Thus shall Babylon sink, and shall not rise from the evil that I will bring upon her: and they shall be weary. Thus far are the words of Jeremiah."*

The mention of the Euphrates River connects with a literal city located there – and reveals the source of the major trading with Babylon that the merchants of the earth will engage in by their trade and merchandise.

   2. It will bring several __CONSEQUENCES!__

       (1)   No more __MUSIC!__

       (2)   No more __MANUFACTURING!__

       (3)   No more __MARRIAGE!__

All activity is removed – *"and the light of a candle shall shine no more at all in thee."*

3. It will reveal the __CAUSES__ for this judgment!

Two things are listed in Revelation 18:23-24:

       (1)   SORCERIES – *"for by thy sorceries were all nations deceived"*

The word "pharmaceuticals" is, of course, referring to the non-medicinal use of drugs, which today dominates the cultures of the world. Back in Revelation 9 we learn of the rebellion of people, that in spite of a major demonic attack, they will refuse to repent of their deeds. They will actually *"worship devils and idols"* and will not repent of *"murders, nor of their sorceries, nor of their fornication, nor of their thefts."*

(2) SLAYINGS – *"and in her was found the blood of prophets, and of saints, and of all that were slain upon the earth."*

Millions of people have been killed throughout the history of the world, and even into the present day. We read of such barbaric acts of "beheadings" and senseless killing of babies by worldwide abortions, and killing of children in a multitude of ways and diabolical schemes. God help us!

JUDGMENT DAY is coming! The greatest destruction ever imagined on planet earth is coming as the Day of the Lord concludes, and II Peter 3 teaches clearly. The entire planet will be burned with fire, and all the molecular structure of things upon which we depend will be destroyed.

THE PRAISE OF HEAVEN OVER THE DESTRUCTION OF THE GREAT HARLOT – BABYLON THE GREAT!
Revelation 19:1-6

"And after these things I heard a great voice of much people in heaven, saying, Alleluia; Salvation, and glory, and honor, and power, unto the Lord our God: For true and righteous are His judgments: for He hath judged the great whore, which did corrupt the earth with her fornication, and hath

avenged the blood of His servants at her hand. And again they say, Alleluia. And her smoke rose up forever and ever. And the four and twenty elders and the four beasts (living creatures – cherubim angels) *fell down and worshipped God that sat on the throne, saying, Amen; Alleluia. And a voice came out of the throne, saying, Praise our God, all ye His servants, and ye that fear Him, both small and great. And I heard as it were the voice of a great multitude, and as the voice of many waters, and as the voice of mighty thunderings, saying, Alleluia: for the Lord God omnipotent reigneth."*

WHO GIVES THIS PRAISE?

Revelation 19:1 says *"a great voice of much people in heaven"*

WHY IS THIS PRAISE BEING GIVEN?

Revelation 19:2 – *"For true and righteous are His judgments: for He hath judged the great whore, which did corrupt the earth with her fornication, and hath avenged the blood of His servants at her hand."*

1. The <u>ABOMINATIONS</u> by which this woman corrupted the earth!

2. The <u>AVENGING</u> of the blood of His servants!

WHO GIVES IMMEDIATE WORSHIP TO GOD?

Revelation 19:4 – *"And the four and twenty elders and the four beasts fell down and worshipped God that sat on the throne, saying, Amen; Alleluia."*

1. The <u>CHURCH</u> of Jesus Christ – represented by the 24 elders in heaven – cf. Revelation 4 & 5.

2. The <u>CHERUBIM</u> angels who lead the worship of heaven – four beasts (living creatures)

WHAT WAS THE CENTRAL FOCUS OF THEIR PRAISE?

Revelation 19:6 – *"Alleluia: for the Lord God omnipotent reigneth!"*

What a fabulous summary of the Bible's presentation of a great harlot, BABYLON THE GREAT!

SOME FINAL THOUGHTS!

In this brief study we have examined the Biblical and historical information we have concerning the identity, history, and prophecies of BABLON THE GREAT. It appears to us that the viewpoint that rests upon more solid ground and example than other opinions is that the woman riding the beast is, in fact, a religious system that began in ancient Babylon that originated with Nimrod and his wife Semiramis. This religious system has penetrated all cultures and nations since the days Babylon was created and built by Nimrod and his people. The Tower of Babel was simply one attempt by people and their own hands to reach all the way to heaven. We noticed that some 24 ziggurats and their ruins are still visible in the Mesopotamian valley.

It is quite easy for people to refer to BABYLON THE GREAT as a past problem that we don't have to face today! Such is far from the truth! Babylonianism has infiltrated all nations according to the Bible, and that includes the Church of Jesus Christ (for almost 2000 years!). In terms of church history the most likely fulfillment of Babylonianism is the Roman Catholic Church. We realize that there are millions of Catholics in this world who are quite sincere in their beliefs and practices, believing them to be Biblical when, in fact, they have little to do with Biblical facts and teachings.

But, to all of our Catholic friends, thank you for reading this (as difficult as it may have been!) book. The Roman Catholic Church argues that it began with the death, resurrection, and ascension of our Lord Jesus Christ in approximately 30 AD. They argue that the first pope was Peter and the location was Rome!

But, in the Bible, the city where the church began was Jerusalem, and the first pastor was James (Yaakov – in Hebrew), the brother of our Lord. It was primarily a Jewish Church, built upon Old Testament teachings and the promise of a New Covenant. Jesus was not a Gentile, and was not a Palestinian – He was an orthodox Jew! The whole story of the gospels depends upon Jewish understanding.

There is no mention in the teachings of Jesus or His apostles about the following prominent views of Catholic priests and scholars:

PAPACY

WORSHIP OF MARY (Hebrew name – Miryam)

IMMACULATE CONCEPTION OF MARY

PERPETUAL VIRGINITY OF MARY

ASSUMPTION OF MARY

MARY AS CO-REDEMPTRIX OR CO-MEDIATRIX

PRAYING TO MARY

PETITIONS OF PRAYER TO SAINTS

APOSTOLIC SUCCESSION

SEVEN SACRAMENTS

INFANT BAPTISM

CONFESSION TO A PRIEST

PURGATORY

INDULGENCES

EQUAL AUTHORITY OF CHURCH AND SCRIPTURE

RELIGIOUS ARTIFACTS TO WORSHIP

MASS

LAST RITES

CHURCH STARTED IN ROME

PETER AS THE FIRST POPE

And...many other minor issues that cloud people's minds and understanding.

One of the most important issues of Babylonianism is that of the place and prophecies about ISRAEL which appear 2566 times in the Bible. It is well known that the Roman Catholic Church (one of the strongest land owners in the nation of Israel today) has been quite resistant to the Nation of Israel and its role in prophecy. The truth is that the Roman Catholic Church was prominent in its resistance and its promotion of itself as the true Israel. It has been a continual problem in assessing the role and priority of the city of Jerusalem. The Vatican is responsible for so much animosity against Israel. They were also very active in the Third Reich and support of Adolph Hitler.

The Roman Catholic Church does very little to teach its people the relationship of both Jew and Gentile in the body of Christ. They are not the only problem – thousands of Gentile believers have nothing to do with the modern State of Israel or with Biblical teachings concerning Israel.

Catholic celebrations and festivals are rooted more in the paganism of Babylon than in the Bible, and they are quite reluctant to refer to the Jewish roots of the Christian faith.

From an historical perspective, during the first 280 years of Christian history, Christianity was banned by the Roman Empire and Christians were severely persecuted. This fact changed dramatically at the time of Constantine who supposedly converted to Christianity. Constantine brought religious toleration with the Edict of Milan in 313 AD. He then called for an empire-wide Council (Nicea) in 325 AD in a attempt to unify Christianity. While this might appear to be a positive development in the history of the Christian Church, the results were anything but positive.

Constantine, though claiming to be a true believer, he continued many of his pagan beliefs and practices and Babylonianism became firmly entrenched in the history of the Church and its leadership. Constantine promoted what he called the "Christian-ization" of pagan beliefs. For example:

1. THE CULT OF ISIS

This Egyptian mother-goddess religion was quickly absorbed into Christianity by simply replacing Isis with Mary. Many of the titles for Isis (rooted in Babylonianism) such as "Queen of Heaven" and "Mother of God" were given to Mary. Mary, a godly woman and mother of our Lord, was given an exalted role in the Christian faith far beyond what the Bible says of her. Many of the temples to Isis were converted into temples dedicated to Mary. The first clear hints of Catholic Mariology occur in the writings of Origen, who lived in

Alexandria, Egypt, which happened to be the center of Isis worship.

2. MITHRAISM

Though few Christians today know anything about "Mithraism" it was very popular in the 1st to the 5th centuries AD. Roman soldiers, and political leaders, including several emperors practiced it, even though it was never given "official" status in the Roman Empire.

One of the primary beliefs involved a sacrificial meal which involved the eating of the flesh and blood of a bull. Mithras, the god of Mithraism they argued was "present" in the flesh and blood of the bull, and when consumed, it granted salvation to those who ate this "sacrificial meal". Mithraism also had seven sacraments – hard to ignore the connection with Roman Catholicism. Church leaders at the time of Constantine found an easy substitution of the sacrificial meal of Mithraism – the Lord's Supper – which became known as the Catholic Mass or Eucharist.

3. HENOTHEISM

Once again, few Christians have heard of this belief though most Roman emperors were henotheists. A henotheist is one who believes in the existence of many gods, but focuses primarily on one particular god or considers one god as supreme over other gods. The Roman god Jupiter was the supreme god over the Roman pantheon of gods. Roman sailors were often worshippers of Neptune, the god of the oceans.

When the Roman Catholic Church absorbed paganism, it simply replaced the pantheon of gods with the saints. The Catholic Church provided "patron saints" for various cities within the Empire.

4. THE PAPACY

Perhaps no other belief or practice of the Roman Catholic Church has received such teaching as that of the supremacy of the Roman bishop. The city of Rome was easily considered to be the center of world government and religion. Constantine and his successors gave their support to the Bishop of Rome as the supreme ruler of the Church. Many other bishops and Christians resisted the idea of the Roman bishop being supreme.

In 476 AD Rome was sacked, conquered by the Visigoths, a barbaric tribe, and the Roman Empire immediately disintegrated. When the Roman Empire collapsed, the popes (bishops of Rome) took on the title that had previously belonged to the Roman emperors, a title that the first Emperor (Octavian, nephew of Julius Caesar) Augustus took for himself –

PONTIFEX MAXIMUS – supreme pontiff. After the fall of the city of Rome, the bishops appointed DAMASIS as Pontifex Maximus. Damasis was from the city of Haifa, Israel, and considered to be the head of the Babylonian religion. It did not take long for the Church to be corrupted and seduced by the beliefs and practices of ancient Babylon that had already infiltrated many religions in the world.

Many Catholic priests and bishops immediately pointed out that the beliefs and practices of Babylonianism were now dominating the Church, and the opposition was created because the teachings of Babylonianism were contrary to Biblical facts. What happened thereafter can be understood by this principle: The Catholic Church "Christianized" the pagan religions, and the pagan religions "paganized" Christianity. The Lutheran historian Philip Schaff commented in his History of the Christian Church that the Roman Catholic Church was "pagan Rome baptized!"

When the leaders of the Church incorporated pagan religious symbols, beliefs, and practices into the life and ministry of the Church, the root of the opposition was clearly the authority of the Bible itself. Recognizing that many of the beliefs and practices of Babylonianism were utterly foreign to the Bible, the Catholic Church was forced to deny the authority, inerrancy, and sufficiency of the

Bible, and instead insisted that the leaders only were able to understand and thus interpret correctly the Scriptures.

One of the basic tenets of the Protestant Reformation was the AUTHORITY OF THE BIBLE over church tradition and its teachings – most of which simply revealed the influx of Babylonianism in its corridors.

The origin of the Roman Catholic Church is the tragic compromise of Christianity with pagan religious beliefs and practices. Instead of proclaiming the true gospel of Jesus Christ and seeking to convert the pagans, the Catholic Church "Christianized" these pagans and their practices, thus removing any differences and overcoming the resistance of the pagans and making Christianity attractive to them as they recognized so many of the church's teachings as being similar to their own.

II Timothy 4:1-8 is so true!

"I charge thee therefore before God, and the Lord Jesus Christ, Who shall judge the quick and the dead at His appearing and His kingdom; Preach the word; be instant in season, out of season; reprove, rebuke, exhort with all longsuffering and doctrine. For the time will come when they will not endure sound doctrine; but after their own lusts shall they heap to themselves teachers, having

itching ears; And they shall turn away their ears from the truth, and shall be turned unto fables. But watch thou in all things, endure afflictions, do the work of an evangelist, make full proof of thy ministry. For I am now ready to be offered, and the time of my departure is at hand. I have fought a good fight, I have finished my course, I have kept the faith: Henceforth there is laid up for me, a crown of righteousness, which the Lord, the righteous judge, shall give me at that day: and not to me only, but unto all them also that love His appearing."

5. THE AUTHORITY OF THE BIBLE

There is no issue as important as the Bible's authority as it relates to the Roman Catholic Church. The Church made the Bible forbidden, and said that the reading of the Bible did more harm than good. In the Canons and Decrees of the Council of Trent, we read the following: "Since it is clear from experience that if the Sacred Books are permitted everywhere and without discrimination in the vernacular, there will be reason of the boldness of men arise there from more harm than good."

Pope Leo XIII also said: "If the Holy Bible in the vernacular is generally permitted without any distinction, more harm than utility is thereby caused, owing to human temerity: all versions in the vernacular, even by Catholics, are altogether prohibited, unless approved by the Holy See, or published, under the vigilant care of the bishops, with annotations taken from the Fathers of the Church and learned Catholic writers."

Catholic tradition teaches the "sin of presumption." It is considered a mortal sin, and the penalty is hell. They use the word "anathema." They say it's a sin for anyone to say that they know for sure that they are going to heaven." This is what the Council of Trent says in Canon IX.

According to the official teaching of the Roman Catholic Church, Catholic men and women are not allowed to believe what they read in the Bible without checking it out with the Catholic Church

6. JUSTIFICATION BY FAITH ALONE

In Canon 14 of the Council of Trent we read: "If anyone saith, that man is truly absolved from his sins and justified, because he assuredly believed himself absolved and justified; or, that no one is truly justified but he who believes himself justified; and that, by this faith alone, absolution and justification are effected; let him be anathema,"

The Bible makes it quite clear (especially in the Book of Romans) that we are justified by faith, and NOT by the works of the law.

In the Catechism of the Roman Catholic Church, it says: "Justification has been merited for us by the Passion of Christ. It is granted us through Baptism. It conforms us to the righteousness of God, Who justifies us. It has for its goal the glory of God and of Christ, and the gift of eternal life. It is the most excellent work of God's mercy."

7. THE IMPORTANCE OF THE SACRAMENTS

In Canon IV of the decisions at the Council of Trent, we read: "If any one saith, that the sacraments of the New Law are not necessary unto salvation, but superfluous; and that, without them, or without the desire thereof, men obtain of God, through faith alone, the grace of justification; though all (the sacraments) are not necessary for every individual; let him be anathema."

In the Catechism of the Roman Catholic Church, we read in paragraph 1131: "The sacraments are efficacious signs of grace, instituted by Christ and entrusted to the Church, by which divine life is dispensed to us. The visible rites by which the sacraments are celebrated signify and make present the graces proper to each sacrament. They bear fruit in those who receive them with the required dispositions."

In paragraph 1129 it says: "The Church affirms that for believers the sacraments of the New Covenant are necessary for salvation."

BAPTISM, CONFIRMATION, THE EUCHARIST, PENANCE, EXTREME UNCTION (OR ANOINTING OF THE SICK), ORDER, AND MATRIMONY

In Canon V we read: "If any one saith, that baptism is free, that is, not necessary unto salvation; let him be anathema."

So many of the teachings, beliefs, and practices of the Roman Catholic Church are taken from the religion of Babylon that has infiltrated all nations. A part of the control of the Church over its people is found in the Catechism of the Catholic Church in paragraph 85 which says: "The task of giving an authentic interpretation of the Word of God, whether in its written form or in the form of tradition, has been entrusted to the living, teaching office of the Church alone. Its authority in this matter is exercised in the name of Jesus Christ. This means that the task of interpretation has been entrusted to the bishops in communion with the successor of Peter, the Bishop of Rome."

In addition, that Catechism in paragraph 100 states: "The task of interpreting the Word of God authentically has been entrusted solely to the Magisterium of the Church, that is, to the Pope and to the bishops in communion with him."

Monsignor Philip Saylor wrote in the Catholic Register: "We speak of the Bible as being inspired by God. That is correct. But, the reason it is correct is that the Church is inspired by God. The Church produced, wrote, collected and approved the sacred writings which we now call the New Testament. The Church is not the Church because the Bible says so – it is the other way around. The Bible is the Bible because the Church says so! A Christian teaching is authentic because the Church says so!"

THE PROMINENCE AND WORSHIP OF MARY

The most powerful sign that the Roman Catholic Church has been deceived, seduced, and infiltrated by Babylonianism is its teaching about Mary, the mother of Jesus.

What Church leaders have said about Mary!

St. Gregory Thomatorgus (213-270 AD)
"With what words shall we celebrate Mary's virgin dignity? With what spiritual song or words shall we honor her who is most glorious among the angels? By her means are we called sons and heirs of the kingdom of Christ. And

who become lovers of her shall enjoy the grace of angels."

St. Germanus of Constantinople (634-732 AD)
"Oh lady, all chaste, all good, rich in mercy, the comfort of all Christians, tender consoler of the afflicted, the ever open refuge of sinners. Do not leave us destitute of thy assistance. Shelter us under the wings of thy goodness, by thy intercession watch over us. Oh, unfailing hope of Christians. Hold forth to us eternal life, for no one lady, all holy, is saved except through thee. No one is favored with any gift except through thee. And no one is given the merciful gift of grace except through thee."

St. Peter Damian (1007-1072 AD)
"Mary is the morning star in the midst of the cloud which shines in the height of heaven with the greatest of splendor."

St. Anselm (1033-1109 AD)
"As it is impossible for one who is not devoted to Mary and consequently not protected by her to be saved, so it is impossible for one who recommends himself to her and consequently is beloved by her to be lost."

St. Bonaventure (1217-1274 AD)
"He who neglects the service of the blessed virgin will die in sin."

St. Thomas (1225-1272 AD)
"Blessed are you among all creatures, because you rejoice the Creator of them all, freeing them from the contamination that is by purifying them their sin, and restoring them to their original state of happiness."

St. Bernardine of Siena (1380-1444 AD)
"Oh woman blessed among women, thou art the honor of the human race, the salvation of our people."

St. Louis Marie de Montfort (1673-1716 AD)
"Hail Mary my dear mother, my loving mistress, my powerful sovereign! May thy virtues take the place of my sin. May thy merit be my only adornment in the sight of God, and make up all that is wanting in me."

St. Alphonsus (1696-1878 AD)
"It is impossible for a client of Mary who is faithful and honoring, and recommending himself to her to be lost. Those clients who with a sincere desire to amend are faithful in honoring and recommending themselves to the mother of God. It is I say morally impossible that such as these should be lost."

Pope Pius XII (1876-1958 AD)

"Oh, immaculate virgin, mother of God and mother of men. We believe with all the favor of our faith in your triumphant assumption, both in body and soul into heaven, where you are not acclaiming as queen by all the choir of angels, and all the legions of saints. We believe that in the glory where you reign clothed with the Son, crowned with the stars, you are after Jesus the joy and gladness of all the angels, and of all the saints. We look to you our life, our sweetness, and our hope."

Father Payton (1909-1992 AD)
"She can do anything!"

The worship of Mary, the mother of Jesus, is the clear evidence that the teachings, beliefs, and practices of Babylonianism are manifested enormously by the Roman Catholic Church.

These questions should be asked of every Roman Catholic believer:

1. Is Mary the Mother of God?
2. Is Mary without sin (Immaculate Conception)?
3. Is Mary a perpetual virgin?
4. Does the Bible teach the Assumption of Mary into heaven, both body and soul?

5. Should Mary be venerated and worshipped?
6. Should we pray to Mary?

If we answer "YES" to any or all of the above questions, we have substituted Church tradition for Biblical doctrine! We are participating in the deception and seduction of the woman called BABYLON THE GREAT who has corrupted all nations on earth!

But, the deception has also affected many Protestant churches and so-called evangelicals. We still celebrate pagan festivals, and focus on symbols and artifacts that have nothing to do with our faith in the Lord Jesus Christ! May God open all of our eyes to the dangers of Babylonianism!

We may not agree with the presentation of BABYLON THE GREAT in this book, but there is no question about its influence upon us all.

Jesus spoke powerfully about the traditions of men, especially religious ones. In Mark 7:6-13 we read this:

"Well hath Esaias prophesied of you hypocrites, as it is written, This people honoreth Me with their lips, but their heart is far from Me. Howbeit in vain do they worship Me, teaching for doctrines the commandments of men. For laying aside the

commandment of God, ye hold the tradition of men, as the washing of pots and cups: and many other such like things ye do. And He said unto them, Full well ye reject the commandment of God, that ye may keep your own tradition. For Moses said, Honor thy father and thy mother; and, Whoso curseth father or mother, let him die the death. But ye say, If a man shall say to his father or mother, It is Corban, that is to say, a gift, by whatsoever thou mightest be profited by me; he shall be free. And ye suffer him no more to do aught for his father or his mother; making the word of God of none effect through your tradition, which ye have delivered: and many such like things ye do."

The Apostle Paul wrote in Colossians 2:8-10: *"Beware lest any man spoil you through philosophy and vain deceit, after the tradition of men, after the rudiments of the world, and not after Christ. For in Him dwelleth all the fullness of the Godhead bodily. And ye are complete in Him, which is the Head of all principality and power."*

Again, Paul wrote in II Timothy 4:1-8 (his last letter) the following words of warning:

"I charge thee therefore before God, and the Lord Jesus Christ, Who shall judge the quick and the dead at His appearing and His kingdom; Preach the word; be instant in season, out of season; reprove, rebuke, exhort

with all longsuffering and doctrine. For the time will come when they will not endure sound doctrine; but after their own lusts shall they heap to themselves teachers, having itching ears; And they shall turn away their ears from the truth, and be turned unto fables. But watch thou in all things, endure afflictions, do the work of an evangelist, make full proof of thy ministry. For I am now ready to be offered, and the time of my departure is at hand. I have fought a good fight, I have finished my course, I have kept the faith: Henceforth there is laid up for me, a crown of righteousness, which the Lord, the righteous Judge, shall give me at that day: and not to me only, but unto all them also that love His appearing."

A serious part of our problem today in recognizing the dangers and deceptions of Babylonianism is the lack of teaching the Bible in the pulpits of our churches. Many pastors no longer teach systematically and expositionally through the books of the Bible. Our motto should be "THE BIBLE, THE WHOLE BIBLE, AND NOTHING BUT THE BIBLE." However, the undermining of the Bible's inspiration, inerrancy, and authority, is taking place week after week as pastors choose more modern and contemporary scriptures that cause people to lose their confidence and dependency upon the Word of God. Pastors don't make the Bible powerful; it already IS the power of God unto salvation to everyone who believes the truth about the life, death, burial, resurrection, ascension of our blessed Lord and His promise to come again!

BIBLIOGRAPHY

Alford, Henry. *Word Studies in the New Testament, vol. 4.*
Chicago: *Moody Press,* 1958.

Ames, A. H. *The Revelation of St. John the Divine.* New
York: Eaton & Mains, 1897

Atkinson, Benjamin F. *The Revelation of Jesus Christ.*
Louisville: Herald Press, 1939

Augustine. *The City of God. The Fathers of the Church.* Trans. Walsh and Monhan.
New York: Fathers of the Church, 1952

Barnes, Albert. *Notes, Explanatory and Practical, on the Book of Revelation.*
New York: Harper & Brothers, 1851.

Barnhouse, Donald Grey. *Revelation:* Grand Rapids:
Zondervan Publishing House, 1971.

Bennett, Edward. *The Visions of John in Patmos.* London: A.S. Rouse, 1892

Blackstone, William E. *Jesus is Coming.* Old Tappan, NJ. Fleming H. Revell Co., 1908

Buis, Harry. *The Book of Revelation.* Philadelphia: The Presbyterian and Reformed Publishing Co., 1960.

Chafer, L.S. *Systematic Theology.* Dallas: Dallas Seminary Press. 1947.

Corbin, Bruce. *The Book of Revelation.* Grand Rapids: Zondervan Publishing House, 1938.

Cox, Clyde C. *Apocalyptic Commentary.* Cleveland, TN. Pathway Press, 1959.

Criswell, W.A. *Expository Sermons on Revelation.* Grand Rapids: Zondervan Publishing House, 1962.

Culver, Robert. *"Daniel and the Latter Days."* Old Tappan, NJ. Fleming H. Revell Co., 1954

Darby, J.N. *Notes on the Apocalypse.* London: G. Morrish, 1842.

Davis, George W. *The Patmos Vision.* Los Angeles: McBride Printing Co., 1915.

Dyer, Charles. *The Rise of Babylon.* Chicago: Moody Press, 2006.

Evans, William. *Christ's Last Message to His Church.* Old Tappan, NJ: Fleming H. Revell Co. 1926.

Fruchtenbaum, Arnold G. *Footsteps of the Messiah*. San Antonio: Ariel Press, 1982

Gaebelein, Arno C. *The Revelation*. New York: Our Hope Publication Office, 1915.

Graham, Billy. *Approaching Hoofbeats: The Four Horsemen of the Apocalypse*. Waco: Word Publishing Co., 1983.

Gromacki, Robert G. *Are these the Last Days?* Schaumburg, Ill. Regular Baptist Press, 1970.

Hindson, Edward. *Popular Prophecy Commentary*. Eugene: Harvest Publications, 2006.

Hislop, Alexander. *The Two Babylons*. New York: Loizeaux Brothers, 1943.

Hocking, David. *Daniel*. Tustin: HFT Publications, 2006.

_____. *The Book of Revelation – Understanding the Future*. Tustin: HFT Publications, 2014.

_____. *The Day of the Lord is Coming!* Tustin: HFT Publications, 2013

_____. *Visions of the Future* (Zechariah) Tustin: HFT Publications, 2000.

Ironside, H.A. *Lectures on the Book of Revelation*. Loizeaux Brothers, 1930

Kelly, William. *Lectures on the Book of Revelation*. London: W. H. Broom, 1974.

Ladd, George F. *A Commentary on the Revelation of John*. Grand Rapids: Wm. B. Eerdmans Publishing Co., 1972

LaHaye, Tim. F. *Revelation Illustrated and Made Plain*. La Verne: El Camino Press, 1973.

Lindsay, Hal. *The Late Great Planet Earth*. Grand Rapids: Zondervan Publishing House, 1970,

_____. *There's a New World Coming*. Santa Ana: Vision House, 1973

MacArthur, Jack. *Expositional Commentary on Revelation*. Eugene: Certain Sound Publishing Co., 1973

MacArthur, John. *MacArthur Commentary* (Revelation) Chicago: Moody Press, 1999.

McGee, J. Vernon. *Reveling through Revelation*. Los Angeles: Church of the Open Door, n.d.

Morgan, G. Campbell. *The Letters of our Lord.* Old Tappan, NJ: *Fleming H. Revell Co.* n.d.

Newell, William R. *The Book of Revelation.* Chicago: Moody Press, 1935.

Pentecost, J. Dwight. *Things to Come.* Grand Rapids: Zondervan Publishing House, 1958.

Pink, Arthur W. *The Antichrist.* Swengel: Bible Truth Depot, 1923

Ramsay, W. M. *The Letters to the Seven Churches.* London: Ho & Stoughton, 1904

Reagan, David. *Wrath and Glory.* Green Forest, AR: New Leaf Press, 2001.

_____. *God's Plan for the Ages.* McKinney, TX: Lamb & Lion Ministries, 2005.

Robertson, A. T. *Word Pictures in the New Testament – v. 4* New York: Harper & Brothers, Publishers, 1933

Ryrie, Charles Caldwell. *Revelation.* Chicago: Moody Press, 1968.

Seiss, Joseph A. *The Apocalypse.* Grand Rapids: Zondervan Publishing House, 1957.

Smith, J. B. *A Revelation of Jesus Christ.* Scottdale, PA: *Herald Press,* 1961.

Smith, Wilbur. *Revelation* (Wycliffe Bible Commentary) Chicago: *Pfeiffer and Harrison,* 1962

Strauss, Lehman. *The Book of Revelation.* Neptune: Loizeaux Brothers, 1964

Swete, B.H. *The Apocalypse of St. John.* Grand Rapids: Wm. B. Eerdmans Publishing Co., n.d.

Talbot, Louis T. *The Revelation of Jesus Christ:* Los Angeles: Church of the Open Door, 19237.

Tan, Paul Lee. *The Interpretation of Prophecy.* Winona Lake: BMH Books, Inc., 1974.

Tenney, Merrill C. *The Book of Revelation.* Grand Rapids: Baker Book House, 1963.

_____. *Interpreting Revelation.* Grand Rapids: Wm. B. Eerdmans Publishing Co., 1957

Trench, Richard Chenevix. *Commentary on the Epistles to the seven Churches.* New York: Charles Scribner & Co., 1872

Vaughan, C. J. *Lectures on the Revelation of John.* London: Macmillan and Co., 1870.

Walvoord, John F. *The Millennial Kingdom.* Grand Rapids: Zondervan Publishing House, 1959.

_____. *The Blessed Hope and the Tribulation.* Grand Rapids: Zondervan Publishing House, 1976

_____. *The Revelation of Jesus Christ.* Chicago: Moody Press, 1966.

_____. *The Nations in Prophecy.* Grand Rapids: Zondervan Publishing House, 1967.

_____. *The Church in Prophecy.* Grand Rapids: Zondervan Publishing House, 1964.

West, Nathaniel. *The Thousand Years.* Fincastle: Scripture Truth Book Co. n.d.

Wuest, Kenneth. *Prophetic Light in the Present Darkness* Grand Rapids: Wm. B. Eerdmans Publishing Co., 1955.